# DEDICATION

To Carolyn Tyler

# Contents

# PREFACE

I would like to share my life's speed bumps with you. If you *are a Christian*, I hope that your faith will be strengthened. If you are *not yet a Christian*, I hope that you will realize that God really does exist, that He is merciful, and that He never deserts you. Not only that, I hope you realize that God dearly loves you through all your speed bumps. Join me as we travel through this bump-filled road we call life.

As I began writing this book, I first asked myself, "What are the most important, most life-changing, and most momentous moments in my life?" Thirty stories immediately came to mind. These stories are not all sad. Some are wonderful, and some are somewhere in between. *Speed Bumps on the Way to Heaven* is focused on exploring these thirty ways that God changed the course of my life. These thirty speed bumps span my entire life, beginning when I was a pre-teen and ending when I was in my late fifties. The issues and topics included are the moments when I:

1. Realized my mother was flawed
2. Discovered my grandfather was not what he seemed
3. Learned that perception did not equal reality
4. Became aware of my own frustrating limitations
5. Carelessly hurt my mother
6. Figured out how to finance my college education

7

7. Stopped to pray as never before
8. Received an answer to my prayer
9. Knew who my husband would be
10. Feared I might go hungry
11. Married
12. Was Alone
13. Dealt with my mother's suicide
14. Became a first-time home owner
15. Began dealing with strange health issues
16. Began dealing with pain
17. Faced the harsh reality that I would have to continue dealing with pain
18. Began teaching piano lessons
19. Began a new career
20. Became a Bible School teacher
21. Began defining my adult child/father relationship
22. Decided to remain childless
23. Became a public sector employee
24. Hiked the Grand Canyon
25. Moved to a newer house
26. Could no longer be a public sector employee
27. Became a private sector employee
28. Came face-to-face with my father's aging
29. Became a long-distance commuter
30. Was impacted by my stepmother's dementia

In the chapters that follow, I use speed bumps to mark and describe each of these life-changing moments. Each chapter includes:

- A prayer—it prepares the reader for the subject matter of the chapter.

- A diary—this is the story, the speed bump, as if it happened yesterday, or even that same day, that moment, *without the advantage of hindsight.* I did not actually write a diary spanning my entire life. Nor are the entries written in the book taken from times when I actually did keep a diary. I chose to use diary entries solely to sharpen the reader's awareness that the writer (me) is experiencing the events then and there without well thought out logical thoughts but rather initial, puzzled, and often downright confused reactions. The first story, for example, is told as if I am a pre-teenager. The reader should envision the pre-teenager. The last story is told at the point where I am a fifty-something dealing with my aging father. Each story is told in the order it happens. In some cases, there are years between stories. In other cases, there is only a day or two. Whether wonderful or terrible, they all describe a drastic change.

- A discussion of the speed bump—in this section, the speed bump is described, *with the benefit of hindsight.* There are corresponding biblical stories and/or verses, which highlight the Bible's relevance, helpfulness, and meaningfulness with respect to the subject. Old Testament stories are prevalent due to the abundance of Old Testament stories, but New Testament stories and passages are also used.

- A personal section—this section asks whether the reader, you personally, has experienced any similar speed bumps. The assumption is that most adults will easily be able to think of similar experiences. Younger readers may not. Please *do* encourage young girls to read this book, though, because it will prepare them to overcome their upcoming speed bumps.

- A section taken from the life of Jesus—it describes a situation where Jesus experiences something similar and to a much greater level and reduces the subject matter to its proper perspective as it is being compared to Jesus and His life.

# ACKNOWLEDGMENT

I would like to thank the women of the Ventura Church of Christ for their help with this book. During the preparation period, I taught a 30-week woman's class in which we discussed each chapter. Members of the class were extremely helpful in so many ways. They made it clear to me that the early draft version needed work and gave me insights into the subject matter of each chapter that helped me move forward to the next phase. I fear leaving some out, but included among the class members were, Skye Tollefson, Claudia Prado, Denette Alstot, Joanie Marcum, Betty Van Amon, Deanna Hodges and Odessa Hull. I am deeply grateful to each one. These women endured the hard job of reading through and discussing my earliest drafts.

Through each phase, from earliest drafts to the finalized version, there were people who read and provided their views for moving the book forward. These include Betty Schulze, Dee Hathway, Martin McCorkle, Corrine Reagan, Denise McCorkle, Teri McCorkle, Crystal Rabe, Linda Oliver and Karen Collier. I am thankful for each one of them.

Pat Gibson and Thomas Knouse were my editors. They gave me the courage to actually submit my manuscript to a publisher. Thank you both from the bottom of my heart.

I must include a very special "Thank You" for Linda Howard. She wrote the poem "Memories of my Father" free of charge never anticipating that I would include it in a book. When I told her I was going to include it in this book and asked her permission, she just said, "That is yours." Linda is not only very talented, but also is a truly wonderful woman.

Finally, Carolyn Tyler mentored me every step of the way. I had an idea and wrote the manuscript. She took the idea and directed my thinking and writing ever forward. She is the one who inspired the title which led to rethinking each chapter in terms of Speed Bumps on the Way to Heaven. There are not enough ways I can thank her.

But without a doubt my greatest thanks go to my husband, Paul, who supported me throughout the entire process. What a blessing he has been, not only for this book, but for our entire marriage. I continuously thank God for him.

# INTRODUCTION

The suicide note my mom wrote me just prior to her passing was in my hand once again. I had not looked at it since I placed it in the box I had labeled "MOM" decades earlier. It was not that the box had items related to my mom, but rather, it was labeled "MOM" because I always wanted to remember where the precious last words from my mother to me were so they would never accidentally be thrown away during a fit of closet cleaning. On this day, I had thought I would do just that. I was a newly retired woman, and after working full-time for forty-plus years, I was ready to take new interest in cleaning out the clutter accumulated through so many years of neglect.

I had laid the note atop the box of stuff I had kept from my childhood. My mother had folded the note in precise thirds as if it might have been intended to be placed in an envelope. There were four notes, one for each of my brothers, one for me, and one for my father. My mother had folded all the notes individually as if she had written one, folded it, then the next, folded it, until she was finished with all four notes. Each note was specific to each of us. All the notes were handwritten in what was, without any doubt, her handwriting. Every written line was perfectly straight with no indication of any wobble even though the notes were written on an unlined 8 ½ by 11 blank piece of white paper. There were no smudges on the pages or any other indication of tears or second thoughts.

My father didn't find the notes until a week after her suicide because she placed the notes in a container above the refrigerator. By doing that, she knew that the police or any eyes other than our own would not be the first to see them. It would also allow us some time to deal with the awful shock before we read it for ourselves in her own words. None of us would be suspected of foul play. Even if there were some initial police inquiries, those would be squelched before any of us would be persons of interest. She had planned everything very carefully, as she always had throughout her shortened life.

Other items were inside the box. The diary I kept during the years when I met, dated, and fell in love with my husband was there. The 1970 edition of the Penryn Panther yearbook with pictures of me and my elementary school graduating class was there. The 1974 edition of the Del Oro High School yearbook with the pictures of me and my high school graduating class was there. The flyer from the Ice Capades my husband, then my boyfriend, and I attended was there. Happier memories flooded into my torn-up soul.

More of my speed bumps, the ways God was leading me to heaven and continues leading me to heaven, flooded over me. There were happy speed bumps where I slowed down to enjoy the scenery along the way. There were sad speed bumps where I encountered huge obstacles along the way. All the speed bumps, good or bad, happy or sad, changed everything that followed.

The first speed bump occurred when I was eleven.

# SECTION 1

# GIRL

# 1

## A Shattered Ivory Tower

Dear Heavenly Father, if it be Your will, let mothers and daughters find reconciliation when understanding is incomplete and judgment is flawed. In Christ's name, amen.

Summer 1968, Age: 11

Dear Diary,

Yesterday was supposed to be the biggest day ever because yesterday my family finally moved from Olivehurst, California, to Penryn, California. Olivehurst is a small town about an hour from Sacramento, California, where I've lived with my mother, father, and two younger brothers, Patrick and Martin, for as long as I can remember. My father works for a grocery store a few miles away from the old house. My mother is a stay-at-home mom. The Olivehurst house was a tract house with a white picket fence in the front yard. It had a swing set and a big weeping willow tree in the backyard. It was the best backyard in the neighborhood, but the one in Penryn was so much better.

Three years ago, my parents bought three acres of a plum orchard in Penryn, a very small town in the foothills of the Sierra Nevadas. Their dream of building a house on their Penryn land had finally come true. I was there when they decided exactly where the kitchen window was going to be, right in front of the big granite rock formation on our land. We aren't bringing our swing set to Penryn. I'm going to be playing on my very own nature-made, granite swing set!

I am a little sad to leave the church we attend in Olivehurst, though. I loved going there. I loved the songs we sang. I loved praying for my friends. We usually were there at least three times a week. Brother Long, as we called our preacher, was a "fire and brimstone" preacher. It was because of him that I became a Christian when I was five years old. His sermons convinced me that I was a sinner and that I needed to be forgiven by God for my sins. And besides that, Brother Long tells good stories.

Sad or not, first thing yesterday morning, there was a flurry of activity in our Olivehurst house. Minute by minute there were more and more blank spots where our furniture and household items used to be. I was having a great time playing jacks in our empty living room in a corner as far away from all the hubbub as possible. My parents gave me the package of jacks first thing yesterday morning. Once everything was moved out, we got in the car and said good-bye to our house in a subdivision and made way to our new home in the country.

We arrived in Penryn after about a one-hour drive. Our three-bedroom, two-bathroom house looks like a great big house on a hill. It has a big sunken family room with a fireplace in one corner that has bricks from the floor to the ceiling and a huge formal living room. The kitchen is about twice as big as the one in Olivehurst.

I love it here. Alice had to fall down a well to find Wonderland. Dorothy had to get swept away by an imaginary tornado to find Oz. All I had to do was walk out the front door. The front yard isn't Yosemite. It's better! The granite rock formation that occupies the space where a front yard would normally be is the perfect size for me to climb on, not too high and not too low. It is the perfect size for me to sit on, not too narrow and not too wide. It is the perfect size for me to explore, not too huge and not too small. The buckeye and oak trees that are growing amongst the rocks are just the right size, not too tall to prevent a view of the rest of the countryside and not too short to be hidden from view by the rocks. It is incredible to think that every time I go out this will be my view.

And that's not all that is visible from the front door. Plum trees cover the hillside just past the granite rocks. A mini forest is beyond the plum trees. It is a magical place worthy of much further exploration.

I couldn't stay inside the house for even one minute. I had to go outside right then, and that was when what had been a marvelous day turned into a terrible day. As I eagerly took my first few steps on to the newly laid concrete walkway leading from the front door to the garage driveway, I heard my mother calling me and turned toward her and knew instantly that I was in trouble. My mother, who is normally soft-spoken, was furious and wanted to know why I was ignoring her. Confused, I told her that I did hear her and did turn toward her and yelled back at her, "I don't know why you are so mad at me!" That only made the situation worse. In response, she replied, "Go to your room and think about what you have done!"

Sitting on the floor in my empty bedroom, I thought, *How can I trust my mother? I am innocent—punished for something I have not done. My mother thinks I am a liar. She doesn't trust me. How can I convince her that I had not heard her the first time she called me?* She must have called me and I turned toward her. However, since I was so awestruck by the splendor around me, I must have stayed in my own little world and just continued walking. I honestly do not remember doing that. I only remember hearing her one time, which according to her, was the second or third time.

She is still so incredibly angry, though, that she is never going to believe my side of the story.

end of diary entry

# Speed Bump 1: A Shattered Ivory Tower

My mother had been perfect in my eyes prior to this occurrence. She knew all. She fixed it when something was wrong. She provided whatever I needed. Punishments were given to me for my own good. I had placed her on an ivory tower. This speed bump hurt badly because the ivory tower had been shattered.

I know now that my mom would have been tired to the point of exhaustion on that moving day. What had been a day of adventure and wonder for me must have been a day of back-breaking, never-ending work for my mom. The last thing she needed was a mother-daughter episode. But at eleven, I could not focus on anything except how wronged I was. I felt as if I were Balaam's donkey. Here's the story from Numbers 22:21–30.

Balaam got up in the morning, saddled his donkey and went with the princes of Moab. But God was very angry when he went, and the angel of the Lord stood in the road to oppose him. Balaam was riding on his donkey, and his two servants were with him. When the donkey saw the angel of the Lord standing in the road with a drawn sword in his hand, she turned off the road into a field. Balaam beat her to get her back on the road. Then the angel of the Lord, stood in a narrow path between two vineyards, with walls on both sides. When the donkey saw the angel of the Lord, she pressed close to the wall, crushing Balaam's foot against it. So, he beat her again. Then the angel of the Lord moved on ahead and stood in a narrow place where there was no room to turn, either to the right or to the left. When the donkey saw the angel of the Lord, she lay down under Balaam, and he was angry and beat her with his staff. Then the Lord opened the donkey's mouth, and she said to Balaam, "What have I done to you to make you beat me these three times?" Balaam answered the donkey, "*You have made a fool of me!* If I had a sword in my hand, I would kill you right now." The donkey said to Balaam, "Am I not your own donkey, which you have always ridden, to this day? *Have I been in the habit of doing this to you?*" "No," he said.

My mom felt as if I had made a fool of her by ignoring her, and I, on the other hand, was all twisted up in a web of hurt feelings because, just like Balaam's donkey had not been in the habit of going off the path, I had not been in the habit of ignoring my mom.

## Personal Reflections

1. When did you learn your parents weren't perfect?
2. When were you punished for something you did not do?
3. When did you accuse someone wrongly?
4. What impact did these episodes have on your life?

# Reflections from the Life of Christ

Christianity tells us that Jesus was sinless. His crucifixion was unfair and unjust. That means that we, too, as imitators of Christ, should not expect our lives to be free from wrong accusations and unfair punishment.

# 2

## A DRAWBRIDGE

Dear Heavenly Father, if it be Your will, let those whose understanding of the world has been destroyed find a way to deal with the world as it is. In Christ's name, amen.

Summer 1969, Age: 12

Dear Diary,

I love living in Penryn even more now than I did the very first day I was here. My brothers and I have traipsed all over our little corner of the world, feeling much like Lewis and Clark. We've discovered a swamp and a little creek not far from our house. The creek is not much more than a trickle, but oh what fun I've had endlessly jumping across it, making sure that I never get wet because surely there has to be some deadly disease lurking within its waters! There's a meadow behind our house, where grass grows taller than me. It is so much fun "stomping" imaginary houses in the grass. The tall grass makes great walls for each of the rooms in my secluded hideaways.

Clearly, though, my parents aren't nearly as happy as my brothers and I are. During the winter, their heating bill was much more than they anticipated, so instead of using our forced-air heating unit, my dad had to chop down our plum trees for heating. He is still working in Olivehurst, and since we only have one car, my mom is housebound most of the time. My dad works on Sunday, but that doesn't prevent us from going to church services. Oh no! My mother, brothers, and I walk to a nearby church building. We almost never have babysitters because my parents almost never go anywhere.

I am still shocked about what has been happening in these past few months! It began with what was supposed to be such an exciting day! My brothers and I were going to spend the night at our grandma and grandpa's house. My father's parents are originally from Oklahoma. During the dust bowl years, when my dad was still a baby, they had scraped together enough money by selling every-thing they owned, including my grandfather's beloved horse, to move to California. The house they live in now sits right next to an irrigation ditch that my grandparents use to irrigate their garden and water their lawn. They occasionally flood their front yard, make a fake lake a few inches deep and then let us slip and slide on their lawn-lake. We were hoping that was what was in store for us that day.

During the day, just as we expected, our grandparents let us "swim" in their lawn-lake. It was a day full of pure joy.

At night, I easily fell asleep, exhausted. Seemingly only minutes later, the most horrible event of my life took place. I suddenly woke up to see my grandfather standing at the foot of the bed. He was wearing no clothing. He told me he wanted me to touch his "private part." Shocked, stunned, and now wide awake, I shook my head, not believing this could be happening and firmly answered, "No!" Then he laid down beside me and asked me to take off my pajamas and underwear. Again, I shook my head and told him, "No!" "OK," he said with strength in his voice, "just touch me and I'll leave." This seemed the only way to survive this terrible situation. At least if I touched him, he would leave, so in spite of how disgusted it made me feel, I did as he requested, and he did leave the room. My brothers were in the room next to me. My grandmother was in the room next to them. If my grandfather had been a thief, I would have screamed and awakened the whole house, but this was my grandfather. I love my grandfather. I love my grandmother, too. With heaviness of heart, I decided right then that I would have to keep this all to myself and that I would not tell *anybody anything* about what had happened.

Months passed and it was time again to spend the night at my grandparent's house. As I prepared and hoped for a good night's sleep in the bedroom they had for me, I thought, perhaps it was only a bad dream. We had visited my grandparents several times since that incident but did not stay overnight with them. My grandfather had acted just as if nothing had happened.

Jolted out of another deep sleep, it was happening all over again! He insisted that I take off my pajamas and began tugging at my pajama bottoms. After failing to get me to take off my pajamas, he left, but it is obvious that every time I spend the night, my grandfather will repeat his nightly visits to my bedroom with ever-increasing urgency.

What should I do? I wondered. Should I tell my mother? No. She probably will not believe me. If she doesn't believe me, will I be punished, and if so, how? I cannot imagine. Should I tell my father? No. It is his father who has done this to me. His father is a seemingly good Christian man. My father looks up to his father. Should I tell my friends? I suppose so, but then I have not made any good friends. Penryn Elementary School is a small country school with kids who have grown up together, and I have not found a group that I belong to yet. Should I run away from home? That sounds good, but then where will I go, and how will I get there, and what will I do once I get there? None of these plans were any good. Instead, I will refuse to stay overnight at my grandparent's house. If that doesn't work, I will have to think of something else.

end of diary entry

## Speed Bump 2: A Drawbridge

Whether I should have told my parents about my grandfather's advances haunts me to this day. The fact remains that I easily convinced my parents that I was old enough to babysit my brothers, who were after all not that much younger than me, so there were no more similar incidents. I managed to construct a drawbridge around my grandparent's house. As the years went by, if the visit to their house was for the night, the drawbridge stayed closed, and I didn't make the trip. On the other hand, if the visit was just for the day, the drawbridge opened, and I agreed to see them.

The incident between Tamar and her half-brother Amnon is a story that most closely parallels mine. Her story is found in 2 Samuel 13:1–14.

> In the course of time, Amnon son of David fell in love with Tamar, the beautiful sister of Absalom son of David. Amnon became frustrated to the point of illness on account of his sister Tamar, for she was a virgin, and it seemed impossible for him to do anything to her. Now Amnon had a friend named Jonadab son of Shimeah, David's brother, Jonadab was a very shrewd man. He asked Amnon, "Why do you, the king's son, look so haggard morning after morning? Won't you tell me?" Amnon said to him, "I'm in love with Tamar, my brother Absalom's sister." "Go to bed and pretend to be ill," Jonadab said. "When your father comes to see you, say to him, 'I would like

my sister Tamar to come and give me something to eat. Let her prepare the food in my sight so I may watch her and then eat it from her hand." So Amnon lay down and pretended to be ill. When the king came to see him, Amnon said to him, "I would like my sister Tamar to come and make some special bread in my sight, so I may eat from her hand." David sent word to Tamar at the palace: "Go to the house of your brother Amnon and prepare some food for him." So Tamar went to the house of her brother Amnon, who was lying down. She took some dough, kneaded it, made the bread in his sight and baked it. Then she took the pan and served him the bread, but he refused to eat. "Send everyone out of here," Amnon said. So everyone left. Then Amnon said to Tamar, "Bring the food here into my bedroom so I may eat from your hand." And Tamar took the bread she had prepared and brought it to her brother Amnon in his bedroom. But when she took it to him to eat, he grabbed her and said, "Come to bed with me, my sister." "Don't, my brother!" she said to him. "Don't force me. *Such a thing should not be done in Israel!* Don't do this wicked thing. What about me? Where could I get rid of my disgrace? And what about you? You would be like one of the wicked fools in Israel. Please speak to the king; he will not keep me from being married to you." But he refused to listen to her, and since he was stronger than she, he raped her.

I felt exactly like Tamar. Such a thing should not be done in a Christian household! Such a thing should not be done to me! And yet, it had happened. Twice! After this happened to Tamar, she is described as a "desolate woman." Absalom eventually kills Amnon and attempts to take over his father's kingdom. David and his family would deal with the consequences of this one act of wickedness for the rest of their lives.

Jesus reserved some of His harshest criticism for those who put children in sinful situations. In Matthew 18:6, Jesus said, "But if anyone causes one of these little ones who believe in me to sin, it would be better for him to have a large millstone hung around his neck and *to be drowned in the depths of the sea.*" It is comforting to think that Jesus is even more outraged at my grandfather's behavior than I was and continue to be.

## Personal Reflections

1. What has happened to you that should not happen?
2. How did it impact your life?
3. What would you do in a similar situation?

## Reflections from the Life of Christ

Jesus was stripped of His clothing during His crucifixion. In addition to all that Jesus had to endure there at the cross, He was sexually assaulted. Our Savior knows the sting of sexual sin.

# 3

## A Street Light

Dear Heavenly Father, for the summer employment which lays the groundwork for the future, thank You! In Christ's name, amen.

Summer 1971, Age: 14

Dear Diary,

Hurray! My freshman year of high school is finally over. Summer is here. Every summer for as long as I can remember, my mom has been packing pears. I am so excited, and a little scared, that this year I will be working with her. I hope to make enough money so that I will be able to go to college eventually.

Pear packing is piecework. Each packer gets paid for each box of pears they pack. We each have a stamp with our number on it, and the boxes are tallied up as we pack them. At the end of the workday, the tally gets posted so we know how many boxes we packed and how much money we made that day.

One afternoon, after I had been working at the packinghouse for a few weeks, I told my mom that I noticed a woman who was packing so fast. I just knew she was faster than anyone else, but I was surprised when my mom told me that she is the slowest packer of all of us, slower even than me. I didn't believe that could be true, so I looked at her tally and she really was the slowest packer even though she looked like she was so fast! Looking at the tally more carefully, I found that it was equally true that the people who I thought were the slowest, judging only by how they appeared, were actually the fastest!

end of diary entry

## Speed Bump 3: A Street Light

It was as if there were suddenly a street light turning on to light the road ahead. I understood that the fastest packers don't make any extra movements. They are masters at doing exactly what is required and nothing more. They do not waste time making any unnecessary movements so they actually look slow. The slowest packers, in contrast, look like they are fast because they work hard at doing what is not necessary. They are working hard, but they don't accomplish anything.

The saying that I hate the most is "Perception is reality." The truth is that "Reality is reality." The perception that the slow packers were fast didn't make them fast any more than the perception that the fast packers were slow meant that they were slow. No. The reality was the tally.

Consider the case of the young David, perceived to be nothing except a shepherd boy by his brothers and the soldiers who were being dared to fight against the mighty Philistine Goliath. David was mocked by them and King Saul, who said, "You are not able to go out against this Philistine and fight him; you are only a boy, and he has been a fighting man from his youth" (1 Samuel 17:33). In spite of Saul's objections, David did fight and kill Goliath. He didn't appear to be a fighter who could take on anyone, but David trusted in God and his knowledge, skills, and abilities with a slingshot and turned out to be the best of all the fighters.

## Personal Reflections

1. When did you learn that perception is not always the same as reality?
2. When were you perceived to be something more than you are and what were the consequences?
3. When were you perceived to be something less than you actually are and what were the consequences?

# Reflections from the Life of Christ

To Christians, Isaiah 53 is a prophecy about Christ in part because verse 6b says, "the Lord has laid on him the iniquity of us all." Christ is the one who took our sins onto Himself. How did Jesus appear? Verse 2b says, "He had no beauty or majesty to attract us to him, nothing in his appearance that we should desire him." And then in verse 3b, He is further described as "Like one from whom men hide their faces he was despised, and we esteemed him not." The reality of Jesus was not at all apparent by His appearance.

# 4

## A BLOCKADE

Dear Heavenly Father, help those whose inadequacies are many to learn from their experiences and to find an alternate pathway to success. In Christ's name, amen.

Summer 1973, Age: 17

Dear Diary,

I'm starting my third year of high school today! I'm quite sure that if someone were to describe me, they would say that I am a dork. I wear glasses. I have such a bad overbite that my top teeth stick straight out. It's so bad that I look like a female version of the cartoon character Beetle Bailey! Everyone tells me that I need to stand up straight and that I slouch. My face is covered with acne. No boy has ever looked twice at me.

I have heard about riots in the streets as well as at other schools and that there is a war in Vietnam, wherever that is. I've heard about "Free Love" and how one in every three teenagers are taking drugs and having sex. Some of my classmates would describe themselves as "hippies" or "flower children." None of that matters to me in the least.

I do love music, though. Some of the songs that are popular right now touch my heart and some touch my soul and some are just plain fun. My favorite singer is Bobby Sherman, who had asked in a song a few years ago, "Julie, do ya love me?" and who played a starring role in the TV show "Here Come the Brides." John Lennon had asked me to "Imagine there's no heaven." After giving it some thought, I decided that I love his music but can do without his lyrics. I feel very sorry for him and think that if I were going to imagine anything, I'll imagine how great heaven must be. Gilbert O'Sullivan's song "Alone Again, Naturally" asked if God, "really does exist, why did he desert me?" I can't figure out the answer to that question yet, but I'm sure I will as time goes by.

For the last two years, I have been a member of the Del Oro Golden Eagle Marching Band. It's a marching band during the football season, and the other half of the school year, it is a concert band. I played the clarinet. I loved being a part of the band.

It is with great sadness that I have decided to drop out of band. The major problem is that I cannot march. It doesn't matter how hard I try, I cannot march. For one thing, walking in a straight line is almost impossible. For another, I love the music so much that I can't concentrate on marching. I always forget what I'm supposed to do and when I'm supposed to do it and where I'm supposed to go. For two whole years, I have been an alternate. This status is reserved almost completely for freshmen, but I was an alternate for my entire sophomore year. I would be the first junior alternate if I stay in the band this year. This summer, I went to band camp where I hoped I would somehow get better, but even after getting help from all the best people, I did not get any better. After that demoralizing experience, I spent the rest of the summer praying and thinking about what I should do. The decision to quit the band was clear, but I still feel like a complete failure.

end of diary entry

## Speed Bump 4: A Blockade

As small and even laughable as it seems to me now, at the time, it was devastating. Prior to this speed bump, if I really wanted something, I had always gotten it, and I really wanted to be a fully participating member of the marching band. Being an alternate was not acceptable. I had come face-to-face with my life's first blockade.

Of course, in a very short time, I didn't even notice the blockade and became interested in a host of other activities. The blockade caused me to open my eyes to see the other pathways available to me. Instead of feeling sorry for myself because I was no longer a member of the Del Oro Golden Eagle Marching Band, I was thrilled by new friends and new passions I would otherwise have missed. What a blessing!

In Numbers 11:10–15, Moses struggled with his failure. In his case, it is neither small nor laughable.

> Moses heard the people of every family wailing, each at the entrance to his tent. The Lord became exceedingly angry, and Moses was troubled. He asked the Lord, "Why have you brought this trouble on your servant? What have I done to displease you that you put the burden of all these people on me? Did I conceive all these people? Did I give them birth? Why do you tell me to carry them in my arms, as a nurse carries an infant, to the land you promised on oath to their forefathers? Where can I get meat for all these people? They keep wailing to me, 'Give us meat to eat!' I cannot carry all these people by myself; *the burden is too heavy for me.* If this is how you are going to treat me, put me to death right now—if I have found favor in your eyes—and do not let me face my own ruin."

## Personal Reflections

1. When did you realize there were things you could not do?
2. When have you failed?
3. What have you loved that you have had to give up?
4. What impact did that have on the rest of your life and those around you?

## Reflections from the Life of Christ

Jesus describes His own point of being unable to produce the results He wanted in Matthew 23:37, "O Jerusalem, Jerusalem, you who kill the prophets and stone those sent to you, how often I have longed to gather your children together, as a hen gathers her chicks under her wings, but *you were not willing.*" It is sad to imagine a mother hen whose babies don't want to have anything to do with her, but Jesus paints a picture of Himself exactly that way.

# 5

## A Tragic Accident

Dear Heavenly Father, let those who speak before they think, who cannot undo what they have done, who cause pain to those they love because of it, heal. In Christ's name, amen!

Spring 1975, Age: 19

Dear Diary,

I am a freshman at Sierra Junior College in Rocklin, California. We still live in Penryn, where what used to be a plum orchard has been turned into a grassy hillside because my father has chopped down all the trees for firewood. He has built a fence around our property, and we have goats that "mow" the grass and are loads of fun.

Today began with such promise. I attended a one-day seminar called the Institute in Basic Youth Conflicts. Everyone at my church had been talking about this for a long time, and finally I was able to make the arrangements to go myself. It was amazing. There must have been at least a thousand teenagers there from all over the greater Sacramento area. We sang songs which we all know. I felt like I was singing in the heavenly choir. When the Bible study started, we were eager to hear what the speaker would say.

So much was said, but what got me was when he said not to let bitterness grow and to forgive instead. He asked us to think of a person who we were mad at and then to let that go. My person was easy. There was only one person causing me to be bitter, my grandfather. I had handled the situation and never stayed the night with my grandparents again, but even when we went to their house for family gatherings, my grandfather would corner me while no one was watching and kiss me in the grossest way. That meant I couldn't just sit and read a book and let the family move around the house. Instead I had to watch, making sure there was always someone in the room, because if there wasn't, my grandfather would appear and start up with the kissing! Forgiving him made a huge weight lift from my shoulders. I felt so free, free from the bitterness that was growing inside me!

When I got home, my mom asked me how it was, and right then I decided to tell her what I could not before. I told her what my grandfather had done and how I had forgiven him and how happy I was. However, the joy that I felt was immediately gone once I saw the hurt and sadness in her eyes. All she heard were the terrible actions I was accusing my grandfather of committing. How could I have been so stupid to be thinking she could be happy for me?

end of diary entry

## Speed Bump 5: A Tragic Accident

It was true that the burden of bitterness, which might have enslaved me for the rest of my life, was gone. The text for the lesson that fateful day was taken from Hebrews 12:15, which states, "See to it that no one misses the grace of God and that *no bitter root grows up to cause trouble and defile many.*" The root of bitterness had been dug up, thrown away, and to this day, has never returned.

However, once I spoke of it to my mother, regret, tragically and instantly, replaced bitterness. It was as if I were speeding down the road to heaven with the wind on my back, a carefree traveler bound for someplace wonderful when suddenly I found myself and my mother bloodied and battered alongside the same road. I rashly spoke without giving a thought to the consequences of my words. I was a college student by that time. There was nothing she could have done about what had happened when I was a preteenager. She had prided herself in thinking that she had protected my brothers and me from the dangers of the outside world, but I had confronted her with the evil from our own family. There was no need for me to reveal what had happened so many years ago. My own freedom would have been just as real even if no other person ever knew about it. It would have been far better if I had just basked in the glow alone and kept my mom out of it.

Let me be clear though, my grandfather was completely and totally to blame for the events of this speed bump. Once he decided to expose himself to me while I slept over at his house, he owned all the fallout. If it weren't for him, none of this would have happened. To my knowledge, none of his victims, and I was not alone, reported him to the authorities, and he died being thought of as a good Christian man. I trust that God is dealing with him with justice and perhaps mercy.

The rash words I spoke remind me of the rash decree that King Darius enacted that no one could pray to any god for thirty days, and if they did, they would be thrown into a lion's den. Darius did not think that the one whom he planned to set over the whole kingdom, Daniel, would be affected by it, but he was.

Then they said to the king, "Daniel, who is one of the exiles from Judah, pays no attention to you, O king, or to the decree you put in writing. He still prays three times a day." *When the king heard this, he was greatly distressed; he was determined to rescue Daniel and made every effort until sundown to save him.* Then the men went as a group to the king and said to him, "Remember, O king, that according to the law of the Medes and Persians no decree or edict that the king issues can be changed." So, the king gave the order, and they brought Daniel and threw him into the lions' den. The king said to Daniel, *"May your God, whom you serve continually, rescue you!"* A stone was brought and placed over the mouth of the den, and the king sealed it with his own signet ring and the rings of his nobles, so that Daniel's situation might not be changed. Then the king returned to his palace and *spent the night without eating and without any entertainment being brought to him. And he could not sleep.* (Daniel 6:13–18)

Even though he was distressed, sleepless, without entertainment, and hungry, King Darius could not take back what he had done. Happily, most of us know that the story of Daniel and the lions' den ends with God miraculously saving Daniel from the hungry lions.

## Personal Reflections

1. When have you said what you later regretted?
2. Has bitterness taken root in your life?
3. If so, can you obey God's command to let it go?
4. Can you do so between you and God even if no other person knows?

## Reflections from the Life of Christ

Does Jesus have compassion on people who are burdened with guilt and regret? Yes. That is one of the reasons He came. Jesus said, "Come to me, all you who are weary and burdened, and I will give you rest" (Matthew 11:28).

# 6

## An Uphill Climb

Dear Heavenly Father, be with the young as they make their attempts to better themselves. In Christ's name, amen!

Summer 1975, Age: 19, #1

Dear Diary,

I'm so excited! I'm going to be a "fruit tramp" this summer!

My first year of college is finished, and as has been the case for so many summers, I've gone to work packing pears. The season is over in Marysville, and today my mom and I are off to Kelseyville, California, to our second pear-packing job of the summer. Kelseyville is too far away for us to drive there every day. We will be renting a cabin. That makes us fruit tramps!

It was not easy to convince my mother to do this, but she had to eventually agree that it is the right thing to do. The

47

stark reality is that I need money, lots of it. It is obvious that my parents can't afford to send me to college, and so I have to earn it, and in Kelseyville, pear packers make lots of money. It is the pear capital of the country. They work six days a week and ten hours a day in Kelseyville. All day Saturday, and two hours a day every other day, they get paid time and a half. With the money that I make, I will be able to pay for my first semester in a four-year college.

It isn't as if it is unusual for us to be doing this. Fruit tramping is a family tradition. Both my mother and father had been fruit tramps at some other time in their lives. My mother's family had picked cotton when they came to California from Louisiana during the depression. My mother and her sisters had packed pears and held other fruit work jobs off and on at various times and in various places throughout their entire lives. My dad had grown up picking peaches and picking "up" plums. You didn't reach up to pick plums. You stooped over and picked them up off the ground! He even tried to make us work picking up plums when we were small children, but it never felt like work, it was just so much fun to work alongside my dad.

It is that it has been an awfully long time since anyone has done anything like this. I know my mom isn't particularly happy she is driving to Kelseyville. She doesn't want to work long hours and be away from home six days a week.

She is making this happen, and I am so thankful for what she is doing for me.

end of diary entry

## Speed Bump 6: An Uphill Climb

I knew that getting a college education was going to be an uphill climb that was not going to be easy or even doable, financially or scholastically. Despite its difficulties, a bachelor's degree was a goal I had set for myself. Setting goals and working to meet them is found in scriptures too. The story of Jacob from Genesis 29:14b–20 tells such a story.

> After Jacob had stayed with him for a whole month, Laban said to him, "Just because you are a relative of mine, should you work for me for nothing? Tell me what your wages should be." Now Laban had two daughters; the name of the older was Leah, and the name of the younger was Rachel. Leah had weak eyes, but Rachel was lovely in form, and beautiful. Jacob was in love with Rachel and said, "I'll work for you seven years in return for your younger daughter Rachel." Laban said, "It's better that I give her to you than to some other man. Stay here with me." So, Jacob served seven years to get Rachel, but they seemed like only a few days to him because of his love for her.

Working for a wife and working for a college degree are two vastly different goals, but they both require work. In Jacob's case, seven years seemed like only a few days. In my case, a couple of weeks during the summer seemed more like a couple of years! Packing pears was very hot, exhausting, and very boring!

## Personal Reflections

1. What are your goals?
2. What are you doing to reach them?
3. What different types of work have you done?

# Reflections from the Life of Christ

Christ's goal was to live a perfect,
sinless life and then to die as a perfect
sacrifice on behalf of all mankind.

# 7

# A Rest Area

Dear Heavenly Father, when the way forward is unclear, be our guide. In Christ's name, amen.

Summer 1975, Age: 19, #2

Dear Diary,

My mother and I arrived safely in Kelseyville, California, and are in bed in our cabin, which will be our home for about six weeks. We will start our new job in Kelseyville very early tomorrow morning. It is the middle of the night. Now that I am here, I am wondering if I will be able to handle the six days a week, ten hours a day work schedule. Have I made a big mistake?

Equally troubling is my failure in the romance department. My prayers tonight have been so intense that my words have become a song to God.

"Send me a man. Send me the best of men.
                Send me a man. Send me the best
                of men.
                Send me a man. Send me a man."

                                        end of diary entry

## Speed Bump 7: A Rest Area

My life's travels stopped for a minute at a rest area on the road to heaven. Here I stopped to pray and ask God's divine assistance. I did not know the verse at the time, but what I was doing was exactly what Psalm 55:22 describes. It says to "Cast your cares on the Lord."

At that time, I was convinced that since I had not even been able to find someone who was willing to go on a date with me and I was almost twenty years old, how could I ever find a husband? I was in such a seemingly hopeless situation.

Abraham found himself in a similar situation, only from the perspective of a father wanting to find a wife for his son.

Abraham was now old and well advanced in years and the Lord had blessed him in every way. He said to the chief servant in his household, the one in charge of all that he had, "Put your hand under my thigh. I want you to swear by the Lord, the God of heaven and the God of earth, that you will not get a wife for my son from the daughters of the Canaanites, among whom I am living, but will go to my country and my own relatives and get a wife for my son Isaac." The servant asked him, "What if the woman is unwilling to come back with me to this land? Shall I then take your son back to the country you came from?" "Make sure that you do not take my son back there," Abraham said. "The Lord, the God of heaven, who brought me out of my father's household and my native land and who spoke to me and promised me on oath, saying, 'To your offspring I will give this land'--he will send his angel before you so that you can get a wife for my son from there. If the woman is unwilling to come back with you, then you will be released from this oath of mine. Only do not take my son back there." So, the servant put his hand under the thigh of his master Abraham and swore an oath to him concerning this matter. Then the servant took ten of his master's camels and left, taking with him all kinds of good things from his master. He set out for Aram Nahraim and made his way to the town of Nahor. He had the camels kneel down near the well outside the town; it was toward evening, the time the women go out to draw water. Then he prayed, "*O Lord, God of my master Abraham, give me success today*, and show kindness to my master Abraham. See, I am standing beside this spring, and the daughters of the townspeople are coming out to draw water. May it be that when I say to a girl, 'Please let down your jar that I may have a drink,' and she says, 'Drink, and I'll water your camels too'—let her be the one you have chosen for your servant Isaac. By this I will know that you have shown kindness to my master." (Genesis 24:1–14)

Praying for a mate as well as praying for a mate for your children may be the most important prayer. After all, this one decision affects the rest of your life and generations to come. Abraham didn't want just any woman to marry his son. In the same way, I did not want just any man. I wanted the best of men. By that God knew that I didn't mean I wanted someone rich or handsome or particularly gifted. No, I wanted someone who was best suited for me. I wanted the one who had been prepared by God to be my husband.

## Personal Reflections

1. Have you prayed for the spouses of your children or for God to send you a mate?
2. Are there any prayers that you consider to be turning points in your life?
3. What effects has praying had on your life?

## Reflections from the Life of Christ

Did Christ stop to pray intensely? Yes, He did! As He was nearing His crucifixion, He stopped to pray at the Garden of Gethsemane. "And being in anguish, he prayed more earnestly, and his sweat was like drops of blood falling to the ground" (Luke 22:44).

# 8

## A SLOWDOWN

Dear Heavenly Father, we understand that we can't always get the answers to our prayers which we want, but when we do, thank You! In Christ's name, amen.

Summer 1975, Age: 19, #3

Dear Diary,

I am still in Kelseyville. The first day here, my mom and I found a place in the lineup behind a woman named Luella. She works in Lake County every year, and this year her son is also working with her. They are from Sacramento. Luella follows the fruit about half the year in places like Medford, Oregon, Ukiah, California, and in Walnut Grove, California, in addition to the packing house in Kelseyville. She and her son have a small trailer and are camping at the campsite owned by the packing house.

At first, it seemed odd. I started to notice her son, Paul, hanging around his mom more than a typical college-age young man would normally be expected to hang around his mother. But as the days went by, it became clear that it was not his mother he was interested in, it was me.

Yesterday I had my first date with Paul. We went to the movies and saw a double feature. After the movies were over, we sat in his car and talked for a long time. Even though this was just our first date, I felt completely comfortable. I didn't feel that awkward, gawky dorkiness that was always present in the company of the opposite sex before I met him. When I got to Lake County, I wondered if I could handle the long workday and the long work week, but it hasn't been any problem at all.

end of diary entry

## Speed Bump 8: A Slowdown

It was as if time slowed down, and instead of dreading each long day, I loved each long day because each long day was another opportunity to spend time with Paul.

I didn't know it at the time, but I would marry Paul. He was God's answer to my prayer. The idea that I would meet my future husband at the packing shed was not something I had ever considered. It was too hot, too sweaty, too dirty, and too exhausting to think about romance, but somehow love grew in spite of the heat, dirt, and exhaustion.

It is not as unrealistic as one might think, though. Substitute pears for grain and packing for gleaning and my story is not that much different than Ruth's.

Now Naomi had a relative on her husband's side, from the clan of Elimelech, a man of standing, whose name was Boaz. And Ruth the Moabitess said to Naomi, "Let me go to the fields and pick up the leftover grain behind anyone in whose eyes I find favor." Naomi said to her, "Go ahead, my daughter." So she went out and began to glean in the fields behind the harvesters. As it turned out, she found herself working in a field belonging to Boaz, who was from the clan of Elimelech. Just then Boaz arrived from Bethlehem and greeted the harvesters, "The Lord be with you!" "The Lord bless you." they called back. Boaz asked the foreman of his harvesters, "Whose young woman is that?" The foreman replied, "She is the Moabitess who came back from Moab with Naomi. She said, 'Please let me glean and gather among the sheaves behind the harvesters.' She went into the field and has worked steadily from morning until now, except for a short rest in the shelter." So Boaz said to Ruth, "My daughter, listen to me. Don't go and glean in another field and don't go away from here. Stay here with my servant girls. Watch the field where the men are harvesting, and follow along after the girls. I have told the men not to touch you. And whenever you are thirsty, go and get a drink from the water jars the men have filled. At this, she bowed down with her face to the ground. She exclaimed, "Why have I found such favor in your eyes that you notice me—a foreigner?" Boaz replied, "I've been told all about what you have done for your mother-in-law since the death of your husband—how you left your father and mother and your homeland and came to live with a people you did not know before. May the Lord repay you for what you have done. May you be richly rewarded by the Lord, the God of Israel, under whose wings you have come to take refuge." "May I continue to find favor in your eyes, my lord," she said, "You have given me comfort and have spoken kindly to your servant—though I do not have the standing of one of your servant girls." (Ruth 2:1–13)

In Ruth's wildest dreams, she never imagined that she would meet her husband while she was gleaning in the grain fields, but Ruth goes on to marry Boaz.

## Personal Reflections

1. When did something wonderful happen to you when you least expected it?
2. When did what seemed incredibly difficult turn out to be much easier than you expected?

# Reflections from the Life of Christ

Sometimes God grants us good things in
this life when we least expect it. If you are
a Christian, salvation is the best and most
wonderful thing that will ever happen to you.
Think of Him as if He were your first love.

# 9

## A Wider Road

Dear Heavenly Father, let those who must separate from the one they love for a time find a way to endure the long days of separation with patience. In Christ's name, amen!

Summer 1976, Age: 20

Dear Diary,

I'm on a Greyhound Bus traveling from Chicago, Illinois, to Auburn, California, and I am crying my eyes out.

In this past year, there has been a dramatic change in my life, and that change has revolved around Paul, the object of last summer's packinghouse romance. After our first date, I wondered whether I was going to have just a summer romance or something more than that. After all, we were in Kelseyville, a long way from either Penryn where I lived or West Sacramento where he lived. It was difficult for me to see how it could last once the pear season came to an end.

Our plans were not exactly well-suited for a long-term relationship. Paul had been packing pears last summer so he could make enough money to buy the car he wanted before he started his six-year enlistment in the navy. I had been determined to finish another year at Sierra Junior College and then go on to get a bachelor's degree from some four-year college somewhere.

As the packing season wound down last summer, we were the talk of the packing shed. The packing boss, a preacher, volunteered to marry us right then and there. One day while we were working away packing pears as fast as we could, an announcement came over the PA system that "Number 36 loves number 47." Paul was number 36. I was number 47. The PA system was used to call out the number of any box that was under or over weight. It wasn't long before everyone knew whose numbers were involved. Of course, I was mortified and happy all at once.

I didn't need to wonder what Paul's plans were for after the season was over. He drove me home, and the next day called me to make plans to go out. From then until December, we were almost inseparable. He didn't mind the drive from West Sacramento to Penryn and decided to use his pear-packing money on us instead of a car. September until December were the best months of my life. We went to movies, Golden Gate Park, the Ice Capades, roller skating, and on and on. My brother declared that we were going to get married, but I wondered what would happen when Paul would officially join the navy.

As before, I didn't need to worry because the letters started coming almost as soon as he left. Like the boy in Bobby Sherman's song "Julie," Paul wrote me letters every day. Eventually he was stationed in Chicago, and I have saved enough money to take a bus trip out there. After about six months of separation, it was decision time. He had already asked me to marry him, and I had said something like, "I'll see." I wanted to know whether our friendship would last through the geographic separation that would be a part of being a navy couple. Would I just be a little fling or would this be something that would last, and now I know for sure. He is the answer to my prayer for the best of men.

My tears are tears of sweet sorrow. The time has come to leave Chicago. We will marry, but not yet. I've finished two years at Sierra College, and now it is time for me to move on to a four-year college. Next semester, I will go to San Jose State University, paid for with pear packing money.

end of diary entry

## Speed Bump 9: A Wider Road

From this point on, there have been two of us together traveling life's journey. What had been a one-lane street turned into a two-lane highway.

Paul and I were, and still are, madly in love. There are not too many stories about choosing who to marry in the Bible. People's marriages are arranged by their parents, as in the case of Isaac and Rebecca. Jacob is described as loving Rachel, but we don't get any details of their romance except that he works for his future father-in-law for seven years before being allowed to marry her. Sometimes love is destructive as in the case of Samson, who gets double-crossed by Delilah.

The greatest love story in the Bible is between God and Israel. Here are five passages which discuss the love God had for Israel.

First, God, speaking through the prophet Hosea, says, "When I found Israel, it was like *finding grapes in the desert;* when I saw your fathers, it was like seeing the *early fruit on a fig tree*" (Hosea 9:10).

Second, Moses, speaking to the Israelites, says, "The Lord your God has chosen you out of all the peoples on the face of the earth to be his people, his treasured possession. The Lord did not set his affection on you and choose you because you were more numerous than other peoples, for you were the fewest of all peoples. But it was because *the Lord loved you* and kept the oath he swore to your forefathers that he brought you out with a mighty hand and redeemed you from the land of slavery, from the power of Pharaoh king of Egypt" (Deuteronomy 7:6b–8).

Third, the Queen of Sheba is aware of the loving relationship between God and Israel. She says to King Solomon, "Praise be to the Lord your *God, who has delighted in you* and placed you on the throne of Israel. Because of the *Lord's eternal love* for Israel, he has made you king, to maintain justice and righteousness" (1 Kings 10:9).

Fourth, David reminds the people of his day in this passage how God had loved their forefathers, "We have heard with our ears, O God; our fathers have told us what you did in their days, in days long ago. With your hand you drove out the nations and planted our fathers; you crushed the peoples and made our fathers flourish. It was not by their sword that they won the land, now did their arm bring them victory; it was your right hand, your arms, and the light of your face, *for you loved them*" (Psalm 44:1–3).

Fifth, Jeremiah, speaking for God, assures the Israelites that God still loves them in spite of what they had done, "*I have loved you with an everlasting love*; I have drawn you with loving-kindness. I will build you up again and you will be rebuilt, O Virgin Israel. Again you will take up your tambourines and go out to dance with the joyful" (Jeremiah 31:3).

One day, I will tell Paul that when I found him, it was like finding grapes in the desert. It was like seeing the early fruit on a fig tree, and that I will love him eternally.

## Personal Reflections

1. How did you decide or how do you plan to decide who to marry?
2. When you found the one you would marry, was it like finding grapes in the desert?
3. Do you delight in the one you have married?

# Reflections from the Life of Christ

No matter who you are or whether you are single, married, divorced, remarried, or widowed, you are loved because God loves you. In fact, He loves you so much that He gave His only begotten son for you so you could have everlasting life.

# 10

# An Unwelcome Surprise

Dear Heavenly Father, let those who are hungry find a way to obtain food. In Christ's name, amen.

September 1976, Age: 20

Dear Diary,

This is my first weekend at San Jose State University. I am living in the dorm with my friend from Del Oro High School and Sierra College, Mary Oliveira. Mary and I have successfully signed up for classes and are enjoying being roommates. All is well with me. Paul and I are planning to get married at the end of the year once he is finished with his navy schooling in Chicago.

There is one problem, though. In all the planning, I didn't anticipate that the dormitory cafeteria would be closed on the weekends! It seems that San Jose State College is almost completely a commuter school, and that means almost all the students who live in the dorms go home on the weekends. Mary and I are among the very few who stay here on the weekends, which would not normally be a problem, but for me it really is a problem. The problem is that I don't have enough money for food! I will have to find a job in a hurry, but as of right now, we need something to cook with, to eat on, to eat with, and most importantly, something to eat.

Today is Saturday, so Mary and I are going to go out shopping for what we now know we have to have. Tomorrow, we've decided to go to church at the church building that is within walking distance from the campus. One of the questions that I was asked over and over in my Sunday school classes growing up was "What will you do when you are on your own? Will you be faithful to God and attend a local church, or will you stay home on Sunday? Are you fully committed to God, or do you attend church only because your parents do?"

end of diary entry

## Speed Bump 10: An Unwelcome Surprise

Hunger? Or even the thought of being hungry had never entered my mind! But for those few days, this unwelcome surprise on the road to heaven was the only thing on my mind!

In the years before there were microwaves, Mary and I found something called a hotpot to use for our weekend meals, such as they were. We didn't have a refrigerator either, but we managed just fine mostly due to the 7-11 around the corner from our dormitory. Without any delay, I found a job at the cafeteria on campus. I worked early in the morning before classes started. My job was to prepare the salad bar for that day's lunch. Neither Paul nor my parents knew my situation because I was too proud to admit it.

Mary and I did go to the campus church that first Sunday, but soon after that, I found that a person I knew from my home church was attending San Jose State too, and he was willing to pick me up for church on Sunday.

During my first weekend away from home, I didn't know if I would be able to provide for myself, but starvation was never an issue. It was, however, an issue for the Israelites as they exited Egypt and entered the desert outside Egypt.

> In the desert the whole community grumbled against Moses and Aaron. The Israelites said to them, "If only we had died by the Lord's hand in Egypt! There we sat around pots of meat and ate all the food we wanted, but you have brought us out into this desert to *starve this entire assembly to death.*" Then the Lord said to Moses, "I will rain down bread from heaven for you. The people are to go out each day and gather enough for that day." (Exodus 16:2–4a)

I didn't get manna from heaven, but that job sure felt as if it were a gift directly from God.

That weekend was extremely important in another way because I had definitely chosen to serve God. Me. Not my parents. Not my friends. Me and me alone. I could say with Joshua, "As for me and my household, we will serve the Lord" (Joshua 24:15b). Well, not exactly! My parents could have said that since our household had served the Lord. At that time in my life, I could only say, "As for me, I will serve the Lord." The household part would have to wait a while.

## Personal Reflections

1. Have you ever been so poor that you didn't know if you had enough money for your next meal?
2. If so, did "manna" rain down from heaven in some form?
3. If you were raised going to church every week, what did you do on your first Sunday away from home?

# Reflections from the Life of Christ

Jesus' experience with hunger during His forty days of fasting was exacerbated by the temptation to make food out of stones. He, however, chose not to use His power to fix His own problem. Instead, He used His power to feed the multitudes of people who had gotten hungry as they followed Him and listened to His teaching.

# 11

## A CONVERGENCE

Dear Heavenly Father, from those who against all the odds marry, thank You! In Christ's name, amen.

Late 1976, Age: 20

.

Dear Diary,

I have become Mrs. April Vider today. Paul's navy schooling in Chicago was over exactly one week ago. He is on leave and will be stationed in Vallejo, California, which is about one hour from Sacramento. I have to take one last final exam on Monday, and then I will be finished with one semester at San Jose State. We can't waste any valuable days while he is on shore duty.

My mother has made all the arrangements while I have been at San Jose and Paul has been in Chicago. She sent out the invitations, arranged the reception, and took care of everything. All I did was get a dress. It is a true labor of love on her part because she has not been feeling well lately. Something is the matter with her that the doctors cannot seem to figure out. She has lost a lot of weight and has us all worried sick about her.

So many people have pitched in to help us. Paul's sister made the cake. My grandmother made the dress for my flower girl, a great granddaughter of my grandmother. Paul's niece, Colleen, actually more like a cousin, sang so beautifully during the ceremony. My aunts have prepared the food for the reception.

Paul and I made the decision to wait until after we get married to have sex. We are both virgins and both of us are eager to give up our virginity tonight!

end of diary entry

## Speed Bump 11: A Convergence

A wedding is a convergence on the road to heaven? Absolutely! Our wedding took place in Woodland, California. Paul and I swept in from Chicago, Illinois, and San Jose, California, respectively. Friends and family came from far and wide. It was a convergence!

Unbeknownst to me, Paul later told me that after we said our "I do's," my father, uncles, and even my grandfather took him into a room and told him something to the effect that if I so much as peeped that he was being mean to me that they would basically hunt him down and take care of him. Completely startled and caught off-guard on his wedding day, Paul told them that he loved me and would never hurt me. He was deeply hurt that they felt it was necessary to interrupt his wedding day in such a way, but clearly, he had passed the test since he said just exactly what they were hoping he would say.

Similarly, when Jacob takes his wives, Rachel and Leah, daughters of Laban, away from their hometown, Laban tells Jacob:

> May the Lord keep watch between you and me when we are away from each other. If you mistreat my daughters or if you take any wives besides my daughters, even though no one is with us, remember that God is a witness between you and me. (Genesis 31:49b–50)

I, on the other hand, felt like a princess marrying the king. Psalm 45 describes a royal wedding.

> Listen, O daughter, consider and give ear; Forget your people and your father's house. The king is enthralled by your beauty; honor him, for he is your lord. The Daughter of Tyre will come with a gift, men of wealth will seek your favor. All glorious is the princess within her chamber; her gown is interwoven with gold. In embroidered garments, she is led to the king. (Psalm 45:10–14a)

Paul is no king and I am not beautiful, but all the same, he is a king to me and I am beautiful to him. The ring Paul placed on my finger was one we had bought from a pawnshop. The ring I placed on Paul's finger was the one his dead father had given him. We were not wealthy and neither were any of our friends or family members, but all the same, I felt as if I were a millionaire.

## Personal Reflections

1. How would you describe your wedding day?
2. How did you handle a premarital sex issue?
3. How did you handle the differences between your two families?

# Reflections from the Life of Christ

The church, the new Jerusalem, is described as "coming down out of heaven from God, prepared as a bride beautifully dressed for her husband" in Revelation 21:2. Christ is enthralled by the spiritual beauty of Christians.

# SECTION 2

# WOMAN

# 12

## A Single-Lane Road

Dear Heavenly Father, be with those who find themselves by themselves. In Christ's name, amen.

September 1977, Age: 21

Dear Diary,

We all knew that being a navy wife would mean separation. No surprise there. The exact time and place, though, were completely unknown until Paul finished his navy schooling last May. We only had five months together until he was stationed on a ship that was already in the Philippines.

Today, I have finished my first week living alone in San Diego. It is a place I have never been before, where I don't know anyone, and where no one I know is anywhere near me. I have found an apartment by myself. I've enrolled at San Diego State and have found a job working on campus at the cafeteria. I'm all set to begin this new phase of my life alone in San Diego. I'll say it again, "I'm alone in San Diego!"

I thought my heart would break when Paul left for the Philippines, but I've managed to pick myself up as wives of servicemen everywhere have done from the beginning of time. At first, I went back home, not to Penryn, but to Citrus Heights, California. My parents had finally given up the financial struggle of living in Penryn and moved to a tract house in the suburbs of Sacramento before I left for San Jose State. For my brothers, my leaving home meant that they could have a bedroom of their own rather than sharing one. My returning home did not change that, nor did I expect it would. I was just happy to have a place to stay until I figured out what I would do. I slept on the living room couch for the few weeks I stayed there.

Before very long, it was June and time again for pear-packing season. My brother Patrick and I started packing pears in Marysville and lived in the cabins there within a few weeks. I moved on to Kelseyville, where I packed more pears and lived in a tent at the packinghouse campground once the season was finished in Marysville. Luella, now my mother-in-law, was there too, living in her trailer. Paul's aunt/cousin Colleen lived in another tent next to mine.

The summer flew by, but the question that needed answering was, "What would I do afterward?" Paul would not be back until the end of the year at the earliest. His ship would return to its home port in San Diego! The easiest answer would have been to stay home and live with my family until Paul's ship sailed into port, but after living with my family for those few months, it was obvious that I didn't belong there anymore. In the end, wild horses could not have kept me from moving to San Diego.

end of diary entry

## Speed Bump 12: A Single-Lane Road

I had chosen to take a single-lane road. Many years later, my brother Martin asked me, "Why did you move to San Diego?" as if to say that Paul had forced me to move there against my will which, I guess, must have been what my family thought happened. No one ever said that, but then my family wasn't good at talking. My answer, "Why would I have stayed at home?" That ended the conversation since he had no answer for that.

The Old Testament Law of Moses sometimes seems harsh, but the US Navy was much harsher in our case than the Law of Moses.

> If a man has recently married, he must not be sent to war or have any other duty laid on him. For one year he is to be free to stay at home and bring happiness to the wife he has married. (Deuteronomy 24:5)

It nearly made me cry, when I first read this verse, to think that God had that much compassion for newlyweds.

Paul had been prevented from bringing happiness to me by the US Navy in a way that would not have happened to the women of ancient Israel.

I was alone in San Diego, but strangely enough, not lonely. I was a stranger there, yet felt as if I were not. I did lead a very quiet life though, especially considering that I didn't have a TV or a radio. PCs, cell phones, e-mail, and even beepers had not been invented yet. Paul and I stayed in touch using the regular mail. Phone calls were rare as they were quite expensive. I joined a church around the corner, and right away there were people who more or less adopted me, people who had been in similar circumstances themselves. What I was experiencing was people taking action based on Jesus' words.

I was a stranger and you took me in. (Matthew 25:35)

Jesus had promised his followers in Matthew 28:20, "I am with you always." I had Jesus right there with me all the time even though I was alone.

## Personal Reflections

1. Have you ever been alone?
2. Have you ever felt safe and secure even during difficult times?
3. Have you ever felt alone even when you were surrounded by people?
4. Have you ever been taken in by someone?
5. Have you taken in someone?

# Reflections from the Life of Christ

Jesus experienced not only being alone but being forsaken. We are made aware of this by His words on the cross, "My God, my God, why have you forsaken me?" (Matthew 27:46).

# 13

## A DEEP CLIFF

Dear Heavenly Father, please bring your promised blessing on those who mourn. In Christ's name, amen.

August 1978, Age: 22

Dear Diary,

Today started out as a day no different than any other day, but on this day, my mother told me she plans to kill herself. I know she is telling the truth. This is no cry for help. This is a declaration of fact. Crying, sure that my mom will be dead before we land, Paul and I are on a plane flying back to Long Beach, California, where he is stationed now.

In this past year or so, life has been difficult. For Paul and me, life has been like a whirlwind. Paul has been stationed in San Diego, then Port Hueneme, California, and now in Long Beach. For my mom, though, life has been more like a grinder. Her health has continued to deteriorate. Many doctors have tried in vain to help her. None of them can find a reason for her illness, and she has been getting more and more despondent. I knew what was happening to her but was busy with college, moving, and surviving as a navy wife whose husband often had to leave for weeks or months at a time.

In the weeks just prior to my mom's declaration, Paul and I had been "vacationing" in the Sacramento area. Actually, we spent a few weeks pear-packing together with my mom, Paul's mom, and my brother. This pear-packing experience had been quite different though. It seemed as if my mom wasn't even there. When we finished packing, Paul and I went to stay at my parent's house for a while.

Despite her deteriorating health, she didn't sit still for a single minute. She was not much of a talker, and getting her to stop and relax was difficult. After making several failing attempts, she finally sat down and spoke the words that sent me reeling, that she is going to kill herself. Stunned, I went to tell Paul, who was in the garage, about it. As I talked to him, she opened the garage door and said, "You told him, didn't you?" She and I both knew that I had, and shortly after that, she asked us to leave, started vomiting, and within a few hours, we were flying back to Long Beach.

end of diary entry

## Speed Bump 13: A Deep Cliff

It felt as if I were falling farther and farther down a deep cliff with each passing day. Waiting, crying, unable to find any footing, six days passed.

The following night, as I was fast asleep, I woke up, sat up, and felt my mom pass through me. When the phone rang a few hours later, I knew I would be told that my mother had killed herself. My father's voice was so weak, and he spoke so slowly that I hung up on him thinking we had a bad connection. That was not it, though; it was that my dad was in such pain at having to say that he had just got home from working his night shift and had found Mom lying in the garage with the car on, dead from carbon monoxide poisoning. He went on to say that in the final week of her life, she had taken both my dad and brother to the Ice Capades. She had worked packing pears in order to pay for the tickets. (Sadly, I thought that when Paul took me to see them, I did not catch that she was even interested.) My dad went on to tell me that she had forced him to *clean* the garage and that now he understood that cleaning the garage was part of her plan. He had been cleaning the place she had chosen to die. Finally, he told me that the last thing she said was, "I'm going to have a good night's sleep tonight!"

No one knows why she killed herself, but we all had our ideas. My dad thought she was unhappy because he had to work nights. My brother thought it was because he was a member of a rock-n-roll band. I wondered whether she could not deal with knowing about what happened between my grandfather and me. In addition, I wondered if it was because of my marriage to a man whom she didn't particularly like.

All of us blamed ourselves to some extent, but more than anything, I think it was due to unrelenting physical pain without any hope for relief. She was convinced she had some undiagnosed illness such as cancer all over her body.

"Honor your father and your mother" is one of the Ten Commandments. To my knowledge, my mother has never been honored. There was a service to honor her, but I have no recollection of what was done or what was said. Now that I have had many years to reflect on the life of my mother, here is my feeble attempt to honor her. She was a devoted wife and mother. Dinner was at 5:00 pm sharp every day. She kept an immaculately clean and always orderly house. She could peel a potato in one long piece. She could effortlessly make a good dinner out of nothing at all. She was the undisputed ruler of the inside of our house. She made all the financial decisions and paid all the bills. She was a dedicated Christian who spent years teaching Sunday school classes. When I was graduating from grammar school, I asked a friend of mine what she was going to wear. My friend brought out this heavy gray-and-white checkered, long-sleeve, hand-me-down dress, and I was horrified. When I told my mom about it, so was she. She talked to a few other parents, got the money together, and went to buy my friend a new dress. My friend beamed during the graduation ceremony thanks to her new light blue, short-sleeved dress. I suspect there were many other times where my mom quietly righted wrongs, but I was too young to know about them. I will forever be grateful for all the work she did in preparation for my wedding. I would like to have known her better, and longer, but that was not meant to be.

I know most Christians believe people who commit suicide cannot be saved. I differ from most Christians in that I believe that a person who commits suicide may well be a Christian, whose sins are forgiven and who is saved by God's grace through Christ's perfect sacrifice just the same way I am. My mom's life-ending sin, if she was a Christian, is forgiven. Her pain, physical or otherwise, can only be measured correctly by God, who might, based on His perfect knowledge, condemn us for condemning her.

In David's heartfelt lament for Saul who had just taken his own life rather than let his enemies kill him, he says:

> Your glory, O Israel, lies slain on your heights. How the mighty have fallen! Tell it not in Gath, proclaim it not in the streets of Ashkelon, lest the daughters of the Philistines be glad, lest the daughters of the uncircumcised rejoice. O mountains of Gilboa, may you have neither dew nor rain, nor fields that yield offerings of grain. For there the shield of the mighty was defiled, the shield of Saul—no longer rubbed with oil… O daughters of Israel, weep for Saul, who clothed you in scarlet and finery, who adorned your garments with ornaments of gold. How the mighty have fallen in battle! (2 Samuel 1:19–25b)

My lament for my mother:

Your glory, O grief-filled household, has killed herself in your garage. How the mighty have fallen! Don't tell anyone. Don't tell your friends, lest your hearts break. Lest speaking the words shatters you beyond repair. O household of mourners, weep for the one who took care of all your needs, who knit you together by the power of her will. How the mighty have fallen!

It was years before I told another soul that my mother had committed suicide.

## Personal Reflections

1. Has someone you cared about taken their own life?
2. Have you had to deal with the loss of someone you love?

# Reflections from the Life of Christ

God so loved the world that He gave His son the mission to let Himself be crucified for their sins. Does letting yourself be murdered equal suicide? Perhaps. Does God know the pain of losing a family member due to tragic circumstances? Certainly!

# 14

## A MAJOR MILESTONE

Dear Heavenly Father, be with those who struggle with grief and loss as they must navigate through life's continued demands and as they find joy in living again. In Christ's name, amen!

December 1981, Age: 25

Dear Diary,

This is huge! I am sitting on the floor of our new, or I should say, twenty-five-year-old fixer-upper home, completely exhausted. We are celebrating our first day being homeowners in the Ventura County city of Oxnard, California! Much has been accomplished this day thanks to the help of the many wonderful people from the church we are attending in Camarillo, the neighboring town. We have moved out of navy housing in Camarillo,

California, and tonight we will spend the night in our own, and the banks, home.

During the three years since my mom's suicide, Paul and I returned to Long Beach where I earned my BA in history, with exactly the number of units required and no more. We knew that in one year, Paul was going to be stationed just up the California coast in Port Hueneme, California, and that there was no California State University there, so I *had* to finish my BA right then or I probably would never finish it. One year later as anticipated, Paul's ship completed its time in the Long Beach dry docks and sailed to Port Hueneme. Paul and I had been on a waiting list for navy housing in Camarillo, California, a city close by, and the apartment was ready for us by the time his ship got there. We spent the rest of Paul's enlistment, about three years, living in Camarillo.

I joined the workforce once we settled in Camarillo. My BA in history meant exactly nothing to any prospective employer, but that didn't stop me from landing a *great* job working in a cafeteria, washing dishes and bussing tables. I did have experience working in cafeterias since I had worked at both the San Jose State and San Diego State College cafeterias. Fortunately, after a mere three days at that job, I found another one, working at a factory testing diodes. It was a job that did not even require a high school diploma. Before too long, I moved on to a clerical job, working for a defense contractor. They did actually care that I had a bachelor's degree.

As soon as Paul's enlistment was through, we couldn't live in our navy apartment any longer. Moving was a must! But to where? Did we want to stay in Ventura County or did we want to move back home to the Sacramento area? It was always our intention to move back home to the Sacramento area, but in the years since my mom's suicide, everything is different!

It has become crystal clear in the past few years that Sacramento isn't home anymore. Both of my brothers have moved out and moved away from Sacramento. No one that knew my father could imagine him staying single for long, and he didn't. He has indeed remarried and moved into his wife's Sacramento area home. If Paul and I moved back to the Sacramento area, it would most definitely be awkward for them and for us. It's better for us to stay away.

The decision to stay in Ventura County was actually very easy in the end. We found our house, Paul found a job, and I love the work I've been doing now that I've transferred to a new job, working in the data processing department. Paul and I are, and have been for quite some time, building our own home right here in Ventura County!

end of diary entry

## Speed Bump 14: A Major Milestone

Becoming homeowners for the first time is, without any doubt, a major milestone. Hardly anyone was buying homes during those years due to the incredibly high interest rates the banks were charging and the huge down payments they were demanding. It was only due to the GI bill, which didn't require a down payment, that we were able to become homeowners.

God, speaking through the prophet Jeremiah, said:

This is what the Lord Almighty, the God of Israel, says to all those I carried into exile from Jerusalem to Babylon: "*Build houses and settle down*; plant gardens and eat what they produce. Marry and have sons and daughters; find wives for your sons and give your daughters in marriage, so that they too may have sons and daughters. Increase in number there; do not decrease. Also, seek the peace and prosperity of the city to which I have carried you into exile. Pray to the Lord for it, because if it prospers, you too will prosper." (Jeremiah 29:4–7)

To the Israelites, the exile to Babylon was a bitter pill; yet God counseled them to make it their home. Paul and I weren't exiles in Ventura County, but we did feel as if God had carried us there, using the US Navy as His instrument.

## Personal Reflections

1. Where has God carried you?
2. What did He use to get you where you are?
3. In the aftermath of grief, how did you cope with the day-to-day decisions that had to be made?

# Reflections from the Life of Christ

If we have homes, we are better off than Jesus was. He did not even have a place of His own to call home. Jesus said, "Foxes have holes and birds of the air have nests, but the Son of Man has no place to lay his head" (Matthew 8:20).

# 15

## A Yellow Flag

Dear Heavenly Father, you are the great scientist who created our bodies with such wonderful, exquisite and magnificent complexity. We come to You with such humility when our bodies begin to stop working in the way that You meant for them to work. We come to You in the hopes of help to return our bodies to their intended level of comfort and ease. In Christ's name, amen.

Late 1982, Age: 26

Dear Diary,

Whew! We have survived our first year of homeownership. We knew it would be hard financially, and we were so right, but now that we are homeowners paying mortgage interest and deducting that mortgage interest from our taxes, we found out that we can easily lower our deductions, and that is a welcome change to our finances.

During this year, Paul has been working for a defense contractor, as expected, but he is working the swing shift, which was not expected. I work from eight to five, and he works from three to twelve. I try so hard to stay up to say hello to him, but I am usually asleep by the time he comes home shortly after midnight. He is usually asleep when I leave in the morning. We don't see much of each other, but that means we have a lot of time to get work done on our fixer-upper.

The real trouble that has developed within this year is that something is wrong with me. I get headaches that last from one day to the next. And, if I jump or fall in just the wrong way, I get a stab in my back that nearly knocks me over. Running is out of the question. And my neck is killing me nearly all the time.

I am in my mid-twenties, and it just doesn't seem right that I should be having these kinds of problems, but the truth really does hurt. I believe that my mom died because her doctors failed to diagnose whatever was causing her problems. My confidence in traditional medicine is almost nonexistent. Her symptoms were obvious, constant nausea, weight loss, and stomachache. I just don't understand why they couldn't find out what caused her to be sick. I, on the other hand, am having weird symptoms. I have never heard of anyone having a stabbing pain, but that is the case with me.

My coworkers seem to think that a chiropractor might be able to help me, so I've decided to give that a try.

I remember my father saying positive things about his chiropractor helping his symptoms. I don't have much reason to think they could help me, but I really don't know what to do.

end of diary entry

## Speed Bump 15: A Yellow Flag

I had reached a yellow flag. Time to slow down. Time for caution! Time to look out for some danger ahead! Time to take stock of the situation and take a different route!

I am reminded of the story of Naaman, a general, who finds out from his slave girl, by way of his wife, about a prophet who has the power to heal. When Naaman actually takes the slave girl's advice, the prophet, Elisha, tells Naaman to dip in the muddy Jordan River seven times. Naaman reluctantly follows Elisha's order and gets healed of his leprosy. This story is taken from 2 Kings 5. If someone told me to dip in a muddy river seven times to relieve my health problems, I would have done it too.

I love the story of how Jesus cured the woman with a bad back.

On a Sabbath Jesus was teaching in one of the synagogues, and a woman was there who had been crippled by a spirit for 18 years. She was bent over and could not straighten up at all. When Jesus saw her, he called her forward and said to her, "Woman, you are set free from your infirmity." Then he *put his hands on her*, and immediately she straightened up and praised God. (Luke 13:10–13)

For this kind of sickness, a bad back, Jesus chose the method used by chiropractors today, putting hands on the patient.

Not knowing what to do is a state of being for all of us. We are only meant to know, partially. That is beautifully described in the great love chapter of the Bible.

Now we see but a poor reflection as in a mirror; then we shall see face to face. Now I *know in part*; then I shall know fully, even as I am fully known. (1 Corinthians 13:12)

## Personal Reflections

1. Have you or someone close to you faced unusual health symptoms?
2. How do you react to people who have strange symptoms?
3. How would you react if you were in my shoes?

## Reflections from the Life of Christ

Unlike us, Jesus did know the future. He knew His purpose was to be the sacrificial lamb for all of us. Sometimes it is better not to know.

# 16

## A RED FLAG

Dear Heavenly Father, when sudden, stinging, biting, agonizing, harsh, awful, sharp, severe, burning, horrible pain
sets in, please, please, please send relief! In Christ's Name,
amen.

Summer 1983, Age: 27

Dear Diary,

I went to bed feeling like I might possibly be the happiest
person in the world and woke up suddenly in the middle
of the night in intense pain! My entire left arm, including wrist, hand, and fingers, hurt. Nothing is bleeding.
Nothing is bruised. Nothing is broken. There is no bite.
There is no explanation except that it hurts!

Paul and I are on our first real vacation. We are camping
in the Big Sur area, and all I can think about is going
home. No, I am not going to go to the hospital. We can

be home in about six hours, and by then, this pain will surely be gone!

We have had such a good time. We've been fishing at Lake Cachuma, California, touring at Hearst Castle, sightseeing at Morro Bay, California, driving up the California coast and now camping at Big Sur, California. We spent today enjoying ourselves at a beautiful campground. There is a river flowing through it that is just right for inner tubing, but that is nothing but a distant memory now that I am in so much pain.

For the past few months, I had been seeing a chiropractor because of headaches and occasional shooting pains. My headaches had already disappeared. If this pain doesn't go away by the time we get home, I will see him.

end of diary entry

## Speed Bump 16: A Red Flag

There were no other options but to stop. Nothing else mattered except finding a quick, decisive, and permanent relief from the pain I was experiencing.

The onset of extreme pain in the Bible is most often associated with punishment for wickedness or battle wounds that end in death. King Ahab, for example, will get wounded in battle.

Someone drew his bow at random and hit the king of Israel between the sections of his armor. The king told his chariot driver, "Wheel around and get me out of the fighting. I've been wounded." All day long the battle raged, and the king was propped up in his chariot facing the Arameans. The blood from his wound ran onto the floor of the chariot, and that evening he died. (1 Kings 22:34–35)

I hesitate to bring up Ahab since he was such a wicked, evil person, but his story speaks to the way I felt. Like King Ahab, I was attempting to be brave and keep up the battle. Like him, I was riding in my car (chariot), giving it all I had in an attempt to keep from completely breaking down.

The story of Job is another obvious choice, but at that time in my life, I could not say as Job did, "Shall we accept good from God, and not trouble?" (Job 2:10b).

## Personal Reflections

1. Have you ever experienced a sudden onset of pain?
2. Have you ever experienced unexplained pain?
3. How did you deal with it?

# Reflections from the Life of Christ

Crucifixion is the quintessential definition of sudden onset of pain. Imagine the way it would feel to have nails hammered into your hands and feet. The Bible does not reveal the gory details of the crucifixion. Just this, "They crucified him, along with the criminals— one on the right, the other on his left. Jesus said, 'Father, forgive them, for they do not know what they are doing'" (Luke 23:34). Amazing!

# 17

## A Pit

Dear Heavenly Father, comfort those who experience continuing pain and especially those who experience it in their youth. In the days when young couples would normally be planning families of their own, how does a twenty-something deal with continuing excruciating pain? Only with Your help! Please God, send it! In Christ's name, amen!

Early 1984, Age: 28

Dear Diary,

As I lie here in my hospital bed, tears are occasionally dripping down my cheeks. I have been to several doctors in the past few months. They told me that I might have cancer or perhaps a brain tumor and have sent me through a barrage of tests. Finally, today I have had a spinal tap. Just now someone whom I have never seen before told me that there isn't anything wrong with me. I should be happy because I am fine!

The doctors have ordered me to stay in the hospital and to lie flat on my back until tomorrow morning. Now that I know I am not dying of cancer, I know, too, that I will be living with unrelenting pain perhaps for the rest of my life!

It's been about one year since the pain started. Since that time, everything has changed. The pain is there when I wake up. The pain is there when I go to sleep. I sleep with my arms outside of the covers because the sheets hurt. I can't use a knife to eat because it hurts to hold a knife in my left hand. I can't hold a cup or open a door with my left hand. My left hand is useless. To paraphrase lyrics from a seventies song, "Sleep is the only freedom that I know," so I sleep as often as I can.

The theories as to why I am in pain abound. According to one, I am stressed out because of my job. Or it could be a progression of the shooting pains I have been having. It could be neck, shoulder, arm syndrome caused by my typing job. It could be a childhood injury that flared up right then. I could have been frightfully overjoyed by the joy I was having because of our vacation. I could be secretly mad at Paul, so secretly that I don't even know. I could be angry with my dad for remarrying. According to another, I need counseling because of my mom's suicide. It could be none of the above or maybe all of the above.

Up until now, I've been pretending my mom didn't commit suicide. Right after her death, I had to get started with my last year of college. She died in mid-August, and school started in September. There were no tears for her. I had no time to grieve. Once school was over, we moved again. It was easy to not tell anyone. If someone got a little close to the subject of my parents, I would just deflect and dodge the question. Lately, though, I've been crying, crying about my mom, crying about what could have been, crying about what I should have done, crying about what I could have done. Once the tears started, they just gushed. Many nights I cry myself to sleep, heavy with guilt and regret.

As I continued lying in my hospital bed, looking forward now to the choices available to me, it became clear that I needed to go back to work. Staying at home and wallowing in self-pity would not be the right thing to do! Paul and I need both our checks in order to make our house payment each month. The little bit of money I make is critically important to our household.

end of diary entry

## Speed Bump 17: A Pit

I was falling. I was falling down a deep pit, fast. This metaphorical speed bump left me completely downtrodden. Thankfully, near the bottom of the pit, there was a tiny branch that kept me from disintegrating. That tiny branch was the need for money. How unexpected! How strange to think that because my salary was required for us to make our house payment, I lived when I might otherwise have decided to disintegrate.

The benefits of working are stated in the Old Testament in Ecclesiastes 2:24 as,

> A man can do nothing better than to eat and drink and *find satisfaction in his work.* This too, I see, is from the *hand of God.*

My work at that time was in fact satisfying. I was a keyboarder, a data entry operator, a typist using a computer terminal connected to a mainframe instead of a typewriter. Before there was Microsoft, before there were personal computers of any kind, my company, along with so many others, used mainframe computers for all their data and word processing needs.

I could see the hand of God in it too. What other job could I do given the pain I was experiencing? Typing required the use of my left hand, but touching the keys of a computer keyboard was something that I could actually do. It hurt, but not so much that I could not work through it.

## Personal Reflections

1. Have you ever had to deal with long-term unanswered health issues?
2. Have you or those you know been through a period of your life where life has been reduced to constant tears? If so, why?
3. Have you found satisfaction in your work?

# Reflections from the Life of Christ

Jesus was God in human form, and what did He do in His human form? He took on the very nature of a servant. He completed the work that God wanted Him to do. "My food," said Jesus, "is to do the will of him who sent me and to finish his *work*" (John 4:34).

# 18

## A Little Light

Dear Heavenly Father, in my struggle to define myself as a person, a full-fledged person, not a poor pitiful person, I found my music. Please send others in this similar condition Your guidance as to how they can thrive while living with constant pain. In Christ's name, amen!

Mid 1980s, Age: Late Twenties

Dear Diary,

Paul and I are still living in Oxnard. I am learning that the ever-present unwelcome intruder, pain, is something that I will have to accept. Fight, yes, but also accept. I am twenty-something, but I feel as if I am eighty-something.

I have played the piano ever since I was in third grade. Even when I played the clarinet in the high school band, I still kept playing the piano. Once I quit the band, I began to seriously play the piano for church. I played for the adult choir, the junior choir, and the choir for my own age group. I did a lot of accompanying for soloists too. At Sierra College, I continued taking piano classes, this time for college credit.

Paul and I are still worshiping with the Camarillo church even though we now live in Oxnard. We love the people at the Camarillo church and feel we really ought to stay there especially since they were such a big help to us when we moved. One of the differences between the church we are attending and ones I attended as a girl is that they believe that during the church service, the church members should sing without any musical instruments accompanying them. Pianos are not used during the worship service!

Shortly after we had arrived in Camarillo, before the pain started, we were invited to dinner at the home of one of the elders, together with several other church members. As soon as I walked in the door, I saw a piano and jumped for joy. I had not had a piano since I left home to attend San Jose State about five years earlier. I did have an electric piano my brother lent me, but it was not particularly satisfying since some of the keys were missing and the electric piano is just not the same as a good old piano. After receiving approval from our hostess, I sat down to play their piano. I played the Chopin Waltz in E flat major. It is a piece I learned in my first year at Sierra College, a piece full of wonder and exuberance. I played it from memory as best I could and did not succeed in playing the whole piece, but it was truly a pure pleasure to be playing a piano again.

Not long after that, Paul and I purchased a piano of our own. Soon I was playing the piano for weddings and for church functions, but not for the church service. I had thought of my piano playing as a talent given to me by God that I was to use to serve God and to His glory. The obvious way to accomplish this goal was to play the piano during church services, but how could I do that when there were no pianos in the church building?

Now that we will be staying in the same place for the foreseeable future, the answer became clear. I would teach piano lessons. I would find students interested in the piano. If they could pay, that would be fine, but if they couldn't, I would still teach them. I would only take a few students at a time and not try to succeed at it financially, just yet anyway. I would pick them mostly from our church, kids whose parents were serving God who otherwise might not have the opportunity for their kids to have piano lessons.

Today I taught my first piano lesson. My student is the daughter of my preacher.

end of diary entry

## Speed Bump 18: A Little Light

I still had a tiny little light, and I found a way to let it shine. Those years were characterized by mere existence, work, eat, sleep, repeat. I did only those activities that *had* to be done. Paul cooked and even cut my meat for me since

I was unable to cook or cut up food myself. Yet despite all the gloom, the light of the ability to teach music became my salvation. I was able to move from mere existence to some modicum of joy.

By far, the most famous God-gifted musician of the Bible is the young David. It was only through David's harp playing that King Saul felt better. See 1 Samuel 16:15–23. God-given gifts are described in some rather unexpected ways. Craftsmen and construction workers of all kinds are included in the list of those receiving their abilities from God.

> Then the Lord said to Moses, "See, I have chosen Bezalel son of Uri, the son of Hur, of the tribe of Judah, and I have filled him with the Spirit of God, with skill, ability and knowledge in all kinds of crafts—to make artistic designs for work in gold, silver and bronze, to cut and set stones, to work with wood, and to engage in all kinds of craftsmanship." (Exodus 31:1–5)

Even when we are in pain, our purpose, according to Ephesians 2:10, is to do good works.

> For we are God's workmanship, created in Christ Jesus *to do good works*, which God prepared in advance for us to do.

## Personal Reflections

1. What gifts has God given you?
2. How have you used them for His glory?
3. How have you stretched your gifts in new ways?

# Reflections from the Life of Christ

Christ endured His crucifixion and His three days of burial so that those who believe in Him could have eternal life. Another reason for His suffering was to give human beings gifts. How could we dare to let our gifts go unused, no matter what our circumstances may be?

But to each one of us grace has been given as Christ apportioned it. This is why it says: When he ascended on high, he led captives in his train and *gave gifts to men.* (Ephesians 4:7–8)

# 19

## A STEP UP

Dear Heavenly Father, thank You for those good and perfect opportunities that You occasionally provide for us. Help us to take advantage of them even when they are least expected. In Christ's name, amen!

Mid 1980s, Age: Late Twenties

Dear Diary,

Today I am celebrating the first day of my new career as a computer programmer. It almost did not happen, but the decision has been made, and it is time now to get going.

There has still been no decrease in the pain. Once I returned to work, I resolved to say as little as possible about my condition and just focus on working. During that same time, Paul, who works the day shift now, decided to take some night classes at the local junior college in an effort to finish his degree, so I went with him. I had no intentions of getting a degree or completing any program. I just thought it would be fun to take some classes together with my husband. One of the classes we took together was a computer programming class in the BASIC programming language.

It was fun, and by this time, I had learned that there were programmers at my work. They were using the COBOL programming language. I had transferred from data entry into the customer interfacing area, where during the course of my job, I requested programming changes to our reports and data entry screens. In working with the programmers, I had mentioned that I was taking programming classes. That's all it took. The programmer that I worked most closely with said that he was looking for some help and could train me. All he needed to do was to convince his boss that I was the best choice.

And that is exactly what happened. For a while, it seemed that the best choice would be to get someone with years of programming experience, but in the end, they decided to give me a chance. The reasoning behind their choice was that no matter who they chose, someone would have to teach them. If they chose me, they would have to teach me the COBOL programming language side, but not the business side. If they chose someone else, they would have to teach them the business side, but not the COBOL programming language side. They went back and forth until they ultimately made the decision

SPEED BUMPS ON THE WAY TO HEAVEN

to choose me. Their decision for me was also because I already have a bachelor's degree and I have agreed to get an associate's degree in computer programming, and not the least important, I will not be getting a pay raise.

end of diary entry

# Speed Bump 19: A Step Up

I felt as if I had won a million dollars. My change in career direction from a basic clerk/typist to a computer programmer was a huge step up. It seemed to me as if it were almost as great as, for example, David's, who went from being a shepherd to being a king!

Jesse had seven of his sons pass before Samuel, but Samuel said to him, "The Lord has not chosen these. So he asked Jesse, "Are these all the sons you have?" "There is still the youngest," Jesse answered, *"but he is tending the sheep."* Samuel said, "Send for him; we will not sit down until he arrives." So he sent and had him brought in. He was ruddy, with a fine appearance and handsome features. Then the Lord said, "Rise and anoint him; *he is the one."* (1 Samuel 16:10–12)

In order to survive and, so it seemed, thrive, with the ever-present pain, I focused on anything but my pain. I dove deep into my work and into whatever I set out to do. I claimed Philippians 4:8 as my own.

Finally, brothers, whatever is true, whatever is noble, whatever is right, whatever is pure, whatever is lovely, whatever is admirable—if anything is excellent or praiseworthy—think about such things.

Notice there is no mention of sitting around thinking about how bad I was feeling and wallowing in self-pity. I did my best to divert my brain into thinking about true, noble, right, pure, lovely, admirable, excellent, and praiseworthy things. To me, that meant getting up every day and going to work and giving it my all.

## Personal Reflections

1. Have you experienced a lucky break?
2. Have you been unexpectedly blessed?
3. Are you on the career path you planned, or do you find yourself going in a drastically different direction?

# Reflections from the Life of Christ

Christ's career change was one in
which He went from being equal with
God to being a carpenter's son.

# 20

## HIGHER GROUND

Dear Heavenly Father, help us to serve You to our full-est given all our strengths and weaknesses, and given the potential that only You can see. In Christ's name, amen.

Mid 1980s, Age: Late Twenties

Dear Diary,

It's not as if I planned it this way. In fact, given that I rarely speak in any class, it was not something I ever dreamed I would be doing, but I did, in fact, teach the third- and fourth-grade Sunday school class at my church this morning.

Being a productive member of my church is as important to me as being a productive member of my own house-hold. The question of what work to do at church had been harder for me to answer though. At first, I thought I would be best suited to serve as a nursery worker. I felt it was noble to provide a means for mothers of babies and young children to enjoy the worship service without being interrupted by their crying little ones. However, not too long after I started assisting in the nursery, I also began to feel resentful that I was missing out on the worship service I loved so deeply.

It was good that I found a way to serve God given my continued level of pain. It had, happily, decreased enough so that could use a knife and open a door. It hurt, but it could be done. Carefully and cautiously, I could pick up a baby without a great deal of additional pain. It is true, though, that I tried very hard to babysit the toddlers and not the babies so I could avoid the extra pain caused by lifting babies. Nobody noticed or cared that I never lifted the toddlers.

While I was somewhat resentful that I was often busy working in the nursery during the worship service, I began to notice that I was not nearly as unhappy if I didn't attend the adult Sunday school classes. Most of the teachers were boring, poorly prepared, and obviously not terribly interested in teaching in the first place. I wanted to know about the Bible and learn about God and His dealing with human beings, but unfortunately, attending Sunday school classes was not increasing my knowledge of God. Often, Paul and I just attended Sunday's worship service and opted not to attend the class before worship.

That situation lasted for quite some time, until one Sunday someone asked me to substitute for a second-

and third-grade Bible class, and I said, "Yes!" More time passed and more people asked me to substitute for them, and I said, "Yes!" Then someone asked me to teach for a quarter, and I said, "Yes!" With each teaching experience, I realized that teaching was the work I wanted to do for God.

My third- and fourth-grade class has between four to eight kids, and I love that I am getting a chance to proclaim God's love to them. I have some terrific material, and even if I don't do a terrific job teaching my class given my level of understanding, I am planning on learning more and more as time goes by!

end of diary entry

## Speed Bump 20: Higher Ground

This speed bump was more than just a decision to teach a class. It was a decision to *be* a Bible teacher. It meant, and still means, preparing a lesson week after week, learning it myself, and then proclaiming it. It meant that on that day in the late 1980s, I began the uphill climb to reach higher ground, the higher ground of greater knowledge of God and His Word, not only learning it, but proclaiming it.

God-willing, I will be teaching until I die. I taught third and fourth graders for several years and then moved on to fifth and sixth graders and then on to seventh and eighth graders. I've taught women's classes on several occasions. Teaching and learning about the Bible is my passion.

The book of Nehemiah is mostly about the rebuilding of the wall around Jerusalem after the Israelites returned to Israel after their Babylonian exile ended. However, both Ezra and Nehemiah had the monumental job of teaching an entire generation about God.

> When the seventh month came and the Israelites had settled in their towns, all the people assembled as one man in the square before the Water Gate. They told Ezra the scribe to bring out the Book of the Law of Moses, which the Lord had commanded for Israel. So on the first day of the seventh month Ezra the priest brought the Law before the assembly, which was made up of men and women and all who were able to understand. He read it aloud from daybreak till noon as he faced the square before the Water Gate in the presence of the men, women and others who could understand. And all the people listened attentively to the Book of the Law. (Nehemiah 8:1–3)

The rest of the book of Nehemiah largely deals with Nehemiah struggling to teach the Israelites about how to live in accordance with the Book of the Law of Moses.

## Personal Reflections

1. What are you passionate about in your service to God?
2. What are you doing to increase your knowledge of God?

# Reflections from the Life of Christ

Jesus, at twelve years old, already shows
His passion for teaching by sitting among
the teachers at the temple courts, listening,
asking questions, answering questions, and
amazing everyone who heard Him.

# 21

## A Timer

Dear Heavenly Father, help us to find ways to keep connected with our loved ones who are far away in distance and who drift away from us with the passing of time. In Christ's name, amen!

Mid 1980s, Age: Late Twenties

Dear Diary,

I just now got off the phone. I was talking to my dad. It is the first of what I hope will be many more monthly phone calls.

I've struggled with how to keep connected with my father. The combination of my mom's suicide and my dad's remarriage and my settling in Oxnard has meant that the relationship between my dad and I has been awkward. He works odd hours including weekends while I have an eight-to-five Monday-to-Friday job. A while ago, I asked my dad when I could call him. He just grunted something about how he couldn't tell what his hours would be. It seemed as if he didn't care whether he kept up with me or not. Often when I call, he is not there, and his wife answers, and it is terribly uncomfortable for us to talk to each other. I give my brother Patrick, who now lives in Sacramento, the credit for figuring out what time my dad can reasonably be expected to be home and not at work. Thanks to Patrick, we've agreed that I'll call my dad every second Sunday of the month at 7:00 PM. I can tell my dad doesn't believe I will call him every second Sunday at seven, but I will.

Truthfully, I've always been a daddy's girl. It isn't rational or based on anything special that my dad did. It has been that way since I was a little girl and continues on to this day.

end of diary entry

## Speed Bump 21: A Timer

I had encountered a timer on my way to heaven. Once I found it, I kept it with me until it went off a month later. Then I would stop for a few minutes and rejoice in the sound of my father's voice. I would revel in having another chance to speak with the man whom I loved so much. I would stop for a second and be thrilled that amongst all the pieces included in the puzzle of my life, one of them was that of daughter.

As time went by, these monthly calls turned into weekly calls and occasionally even daily calls. The first calls were very short and full of long awkward pauses, but once I proved myself and kept calling at the scheduled date and time, we found ourselves talking for as much as an hour if we got going on some interesting subject. Both of us continued to be amazed by that since neither one of us was much for talking.

Sadly, not everyone is blessed to have a good and loving earthly father. I know that I am blessed that God saw fit to give me an earthly father that I just adore. Because of that, it is easy for me to adore my heavenly Father, too, and that is the relationship that matters eternally. Our heavenly Father isn't satisfied with monthly, weekly, or even daily calls. He wants us to think about him and talk to him all the time.

> Blessed is the man who does not walk in the counsel of the wicked or stand in the way of sinners or sit in the seat of mockers. But his delight is in the law of the Lord, and on his law he meditates *day and night*. He is like a tree planted by streams of water, which yields its fruit in season and whose leaf does not wither. Whatever he does prospers. (Psalm 1:1–3)

Constant meditation on God brings blessings.

## Personal Reflections

1. Think about your relationship with your parents.
2. And/or think about your relationship with your children.
3. How do you want this relationship to work?
4. Are there areas where you need to work it out between and among yourselves?

# Reflections from the Life of Christ

On one occasion, recorded in Mark, we are given a glimpse into Jesus and his relationship with His physical family during His ministry. Did Jesus have a happy, contented relationship with them? Not hardly!

Then Jesus entered a house, and again a crowd gathered, so that he and his disciples were not even able to eat. When his family heard about this, they went to take charge of him, for they said, "He is out of his mind." (Mark 3:20-21)

Mary, at least, did reconcile with Jesus by the time of His crucifixion demonstrated by her presence there.

# 22

## A One-Way Door

Dear Heavenly Father, be with those who are making decisions that are irreversible and life-changing. In Christ's name, amen!

1986, Age: 30

Dear Diary,

Ugh! I am in the hospital, just waking up from surgery. Pat Gibson, my friend from church, former boss, and generally terrific person, is here bringing me some flowers. I startled her because the hospital people told her I would still be sleeping off the anesthesia.

Unfortunately, no, this has nothing to do with the pain that started so many years ago. It rages on, unabated.

This is about my periods. I have had very painful periods as far back as my first period. I remember telling my mom, "I'm going to go to bed. I feel like I have the flu." It wasn't the flu. My first period started a few hours later. Lately, though, what used to feel like the flu felt more like torture. I have been having massively heavy bleeding and have been passing huge blood clots and have come close to passing out during "my time." Once not too long ago, while I was at work, I passed a blood clot so large that it completely soiled my pad and covered my clothes so much so that I had to go home with a sweater tied around my waste to cover my bloodstained clothes.

After having had no luck with traditional medicine, I hesitated to try them again. I expected to hear, as I had before, "Well, you're just going to have to learn to live with this. There's nothing we can do for you." Instead, they discovered that I had endometriosis and that my ovary was the size of a tennis ball. It should have only been the size of a peanut. Best of all, they told me that they could surgically remove my ovary and that would eliminate the problems I was having with my periods.

I immediately asked the doctor to tie my other tube since the surgeon would already be working in that area. Paul and I had intended to have children whenever both of us were ready. We are approaching thirty years old, and it is clear that neither one of us is ready or ever will be ready. I always figured that my biological clock would start ticking and that I would just have to have a baby, but that never happened. Pain trumps biology. I can't imagine being pregnant, nor can I imagine taking care of a baby.

I can't imagine it physically, nor can I imagine it emotionally. How would I answer my child's questions about his/her grandmother? How dare I pass on my sadness to an innocent new life? I can't imagine having a baby financially either. Both our salaries are needed for us to pay the house payment, so not working is not an option for me. I can't imagine working and having a baby. As it is, I go home and collapse. How dare I bring a child into the world only to tell him/her again and again, "Your mom's too tired"? Fortunately, Paul has his own physical and emotional issues, so we are both in agreement that it is time to tie my tubes.

end of diary entry

## Speed Bump 22: A One-Way Door

Once I walked through the door, I could not go back that way again. There would never be any children. I was barren.

Periods affect the lives of all women and their families, yet there is very little mention of it in literature or even among and between women. One of the Old Testament's acknowledgements of periods is found in Genesis. Laban had found that his gods were missing after Jacob and his household left.

So Laban went into Jacob's tent and into Leah's tent and into the tent of the two maidservants, but he found nothing. After he came out of Leah's tent, he entered Rachel's tent. Now Rachel had taken the household gods, and put them inside her camel's saddle and was sitting on them. Laban searched through everything in the tent but found nothing. Rachel said to her father, "Don't be angry, my lord, that I cannot stand up in your presence. *I'm having my period.*" So he searched but could not find the household gods. (Genesis 31:33–35)

In this story, Rachel's period is used as an excuse to get her out of trouble. Notably, her father doesn't question her sincerity, so it is quite likely that she did regularly have pain-filled periods.

Being barren is thought of as the worst possible thing that could happen to a woman in both the Old and New Testaments. Children are described as God's greatest gift to women. God tells Noah that he should "be fruitful and multiply," a command that has actually been followed by mankind in general. Christians are especially commanded to be fruitful, spiritually. Galatians 5:22–23 describes the fruit of the spirit as "love, joy, peace, patience, kindness, goodness, faithfulness, gentleness, and self-control. Against such things there is no law."

Moments before Jesus is crucified, Luke, and only Luke, records this conversation between Jesus and some of His female followers.

A large number of people followed him, including women who mourned and wailed for him. Jesus turned and said to them, "Daughters of Jerusalem, do not weep for me; weep for yourselves and for your children. For the time will come when you will say, '*Blessed are the barren women*, the wombs that never bore and the breasts that never nursed!' Then they will say to the mountains, 'Fall on us!' and to the hills, 'Cover us!' For if men do these things when the tree is green, what will happen when it is dry?" (Luke 23:27–31)

Jesus is seeing ahead to the destruction of Jerusalem where women and children would be brutally killed by the Roman army, which would take place approximately forty years after His crucifixion. The women with children would suffer more because if they were spared, their children would more than likely be killed. Barren women would be considered blessed by those women who had children during times of great peril. In fact, some women have quietly come to me in the midst of personal tragedies and said, "April, you are so much better off not to have had children."

## Personal Reflections

1. Have physical issues caused the direction of your life to change?
2. Have you been sympathetic to people who have made decisions based on their physical, emotional, or financial condition?
3. In a similar situation, what would you have done?

# Reflections from the Life of Christ

Was decision-making easy for Jesus? He, after all, knew what God wanted and lived His life by then doing what God wanted. Perhaps decision-making was usually easy for Jesus, but we do find at least one record of Jesus being overwhelmed with His own irreversible and life-changing decision.

Then Jesus went with his disciples to a place called Gethsemane, and he said to them, "Sit here while I go over there and pray." He took Peter and the two sons of Zebedee along with him, and he began to be sorrowful and troubled. Then he said to them, "My soul is overwhelmed with sorrow to the point of death. Stay here and keep watch with me." (Matthew 26:36-38)

Jesus was overwhelmed with sorrow to the point of death as He was making the decision to finish the job God gave Him to do!

# 23

## A Large Step Up

Dear Heavenly Father, thank You for those opportunities You provide. Thank You for the chances to make fresh starts. In Christ's name, amen!

October 1989, Age: 33

Dear Diary,

Today I am celebrating the first day of my new career as a programmer/analyst for a public sector employer.

Some of the people at my old job are truly wonderful, people who knew me, grew up with me, and cared about me. People like Carolyn Tyler, who shared an office with me for several years and was a dear friend. She and I discovered a finch's nest that was fully viewable from our office window at one point. We actually stood there, in awe, as we witnessed one of the babies fly away for the first time.

Professionally, much has occurred in the last five years since I started as a COBOL programmer. At first, I thought my brain might explode as I tried to cram it with all I needed to know about how to be a COBOL programmer. Once those first months were over, though, I began the journey to become what my mentor was expecting and within a few years, he had moved on and I took over where he left off. For those five years, my work was incredibly fun, the programming part, that is.

There were other aspects of the job that were not good. I was still getting paid as if I were a data entry operator even though I was doing all the work of my predecessor. In addition, every year, we all wondered if our contract would be renewed by the federal government. About one year ago, we learned that our contract was not going to be renewed and that we were all going to work for some other contractor. That is when I made the decision to look for some other employer. Why not? I was going to work for someone else anyway.

After applying for a job at a public sector employer and taking and passing their test, I was placed on a waiting list for one year. As the year was coming to an end, and still no call, I called them. I knew by that time that they needed people with the exact experience I had, and I wanted someone there to know that I was ready and waiting. After several unsuccessful attempts, I finally got through to their department head, and that was all it took. I received a letter to come in for an interview a few weeks after that.

The proof that my company still saw me as a file clerk, not a computer programmer, came when I applied with the company that was taking over our contract. It was humiliating because a file clerk and I interviewed together as if we would be doing the same job. What a slap in the face!

Last year was quite unsettling. I applied for two other COBOL programmer jobs, one with yet another defense contractor and another with a private company. With four possibilities, (1) transfer to the contractor taking over our expiring contract, (2) an entirely different defense contractor, (3) a private company, and (4) the public sector employer, and still no job offer, I waited and counted the days until our contract expired.

The dominos began to fall just two weeks before our contract ended. I gave my company a two-week notice exactly two weeks before we were all scheduled to start work for the company that was taking over our contract. I was delighted that I would not have to go to work even one day for the new company. The other defense contractor had offered me a job, and I had accepted. I worked there for a total of one week before I got another job working for the private company. I worked there for a total of two weeks before the public sector employer sent me their offer letter. With each job, I was offered more money.

Now that I have finished my first day at this new job, it feels like a good fit. First impressions of my new boss are good. First impressions of the people there are good. All they know about me is what I wrote on my resume, that I am a COBOL programmer. My years of being incorrectly labeled as a data entry operator are over.

I am still in pain, but I am not going to tell anyone. No one at my new job knows me. I will do my best to appear as if I am healthy, something that I couldn't do at my old job where everyone knew me and my whole sad story of doctor visits, frequent sick leave, no answers, and my peculiar circumstances.

end of diary entry

## Speed Bump 23: A Large Step Up

This speed bump represented a large step up the ladder of success. There would be no more worrying about whether the contract would be renewed. A job within the public sector was secure, and there was a retirement benefit that would build up over time included in the mix.

Turbulent times at work, I was hoping, were over, replaced, I was hoping, by a time of peace. I was hoping to be defined as a programmer and only a programmer, a computer professional, and I was. I had earned an associate in science degree in business information systems. I had five years of experience programming. It was time to discard all the old, tired labels from my early career.

I think of Solomon as he begins his reign in ancient Israel.

During Solomon's lifetime, Judah and Israel, from Dan to Beersheba, lived in safety, each man under his own vine and fig tree. (1 Kings 4:25)

The kingdom of Israel gets this welcome break from their warfare during Solomon's reign.

Jesus and I shared similar troubles with His coworkers. His disciples still did not recognize Him as God's son even after He spent three years intensely training them and doing miracles in front of their eyes. We find this conversation between them as Jesus is preparing His disciples for His last days on earth.

Jesus answered, "I am the way and the truth and the life. No one comes to the Father except through me. If you really knew me, you would know my Father as well. From now on, you do know him and have seen him." Philip said, "Lord, show us the Father and that will be enough for us." Jesus answered: "*Don't you know me, Philip*, even after I have been among you such a long time? Anyone who has seen me has seen the Father. How can you say, 'Show us the Father'?" (John 14:6–9a)

We aren't told how Philip reacted, but I imagine that he felt about two inches tall.

## Personal Reflections

1. Have you had to deal with an unstable work environment?
2. Have you had to deal with lack of recognition?

# Reflections from the Life of Christ

As Jesus was dying on the cross, He knew the people who should have been His greatest supporters were not even sure who He was.

# 24

## THE GRAND CANYON

Dear Heavenly Father, be with those who attempt to stretch the limits of their own abilities. Help them to succeed or if success is not possible, help them to fail with grace and dignity. In Christ's name, amen.

May 2001, Age: 35

Dear Diary,

Hello from the bottom of the Grand Canyon! Phantom Ranch is an amazing place where the rest of the world is far, far away. Getting here started with a phone call to my father more than two years ago.

My father, on one of our weekly calls about two years ago, announced that he was retiring at fifty years of age from the retail clerks after over thirty years. There was some special deal going on that he qualified for, and he was going to retire within a few weeks. My response was to say, "What should we do to celebrate?" His answer, "I want to go to the Grand Canyon, and I want you to find out what we can do there."

And so, it began. I spent hours making phone calls, getting brochures through the mail, and tracking down information. I found out about rafting trips, the mule trips, driving around the rim, and hiking. Hiking was his choice.

Our plan was to book a room at one of the hotels on the rim, eat breakfast, take a bus trip to the trail head, hike to the bottom via the Kaibab trail, spend two nights at the Phantom Ranch, then walk up the Bright Angel Trail. The Phantom Ranch was set up to accommodate hikers. All meals were provided, and a cabin with showers and bathroom facilities was on the premises.

Those were our plans. Making the reservations was a challenge in itself as there were very limited number of beds and cabins available. Reservations had to be made over one year ahead of time. I successfully made the reservations for the following April to include my father, my brother Martin, and me, and then we waited for an entire year. We joked that we were all set for the end of April, the month, not me. During that year, I bought hiking boots. I bought a treadmill and used it every day. I practiced walking up and down the stairs at work.

When it finally was time to go, my father drove from Sacramento to Oxnard and stayed the night with us. We left early the next morning. Shortly afterward, I realized that I forgot to pack my hiking boots and had nothing but my old worn-out pair of tennis shoes with me. Undaunted, the two of us drove to Phoenix, anyhow. When we got there, we bought some lunch supplies for our day hike and some stuff to take with us and then picked up Martin who had flown in from Illinois. The three of us then drove from Phoenix to the rim where it was already dark by the time we settled into our hotel room.

Sleeping was impossible as I imagined what could be in store for us the next day. In my half-sleep, half-awake state, my thoughts drifted to and fro. I envisioned a trail too narrow where I would fall for miles to the bottom. How can that be, I thought, when the trails are used by the mules? Oh, but the mules are surefooted and wouldn't have any trouble with a narrow trail. Oh, but this is a national park and the trails would have to be safe for regular tourists and on and on until morning came.

And then we opened the drapes and saw the canyon for the first time. Grand does not do it justice. Immense is better. Spectacular might do it. Really no word can describe it. As my heart sank with fear and dread, I robotically went through the motions, packed my bags, went to eat breakfast, got on the bus, and rode to the trailhead, got off the bus, saw the bus drive away, watched the other hikers disappear down the trail, and took the first steps down the Kaibab Trail. Ready or not, I was not going to disappoint my father and chicken out.

Once we passed the first switchback and looked up, I knew I was not going back up. I was committed to going all the way down. Our first stop was a little picnic area about a half hour from the top. As we approached it, we noticed a group of people standing around. Curious, we came closer and saw a big horn sheep grazing only a few feet away without caring a whit whether human beings were watching him.

The robotics vanished in that moment as this now became the adventure of a lifetime. The weather was perfect. The trail was wide enough. There weren't any steep drop offs. There was no need to fear. I was going to be fine. After watching the sheep for a few more minutes, we headed back down the trail.

We were alone. The hikers who had filled the bus were long gone, specks we could see down in the belly of the canyon from time to time. Our little band of father, son, and daughter walked slowly past vistas of before-unimagined beauty. We walked for hours in the shade until we got to the line where the shade turned to sun. At that point, we stopped to eat and then rest for a few minutes. After that, we removed a layer of clothing, put on sunscreen, and proceeded downward. We were about halfway there and were making slow, steady progress. All was indeed well.

Not far from the end of our journey, my dad fell forward on his knees. Bruised and a little battered, he kept going. Not long after that, I stopped, declared, "I can't move," and vomited. Disgusted with myself, I sat down on the trail, within view of the footbridge at the bottom of the canyon, but couldn't make myself get up. Poor Martin, now our hero, dashed as fast as he could to the ranger station and within a short time came back with a ranger who immediately knew that I was dehydrated and had me drink some water with added electrolytes.

Revived, we walked the rest of the way and got to the chow hall just as they were serving dinner. I don't think any dinner before or since ever tasted so delicious. After dinner, we continued talking to the ranger and made the arrangements to get helicoptered out in two days. My father couldn't feel his legs, and they were afraid he needed medical attention. I would ride with him, the good daughter that I was, and my brother would hike out as planned.

end of diary entry

## Speed Bump 24: The Grand Canyon

There is nothing metaphorical about this speed bump. It refers to the actual Grand Canyon. There was more here than just a hiking trip, though. It was a gift I gave to my father, who wanted so little out of life, but who did want to hike the Grand Canyon. It was a goal I set for myself, one I was terrified I would not be able to make happen. Finally, it was a family reunion of sorts. I really was still a daughter and a sister.

It was definitely physical as determined by how badly my whole body felt in the days following the hike. My legs, most especially, were so incredibly sore for days, even weeks after our hike was done, but I didn't care. Having had the experience of hiking the Grand Canyon was worth it. As a fitting end to our adventure, when I got home, I threw my old tennis shoes away. They had made the trip, but they were now obviously trash.

The trip was partly a family reunion, which three out of five of us attended. I was saddened that my brother Patrick could not be there. Most of all, I was sorrowful that we were missing my mom being there.

In another way, the trip was a great accomplishment. I had carried out my mission with exact precision. All the planning had paid off. Yes, the unrelenting pain of the past was still very much present. I had decided, though, to throw caution to the wind so that I could do this for my dad, but I wasn't at all sure that I would be able to do it given my physical condition. Surprisingly enough, there were times during the hike when the pain abated, supplanted briefly by a hiker's rush.

Martin wrote about this story in his book *Walk with Me*. From his perspective, however, this day was not a great, marvelous, spectacular success. From his perspective, this day was a terrible, horrible, miserable failure. His book is well worth reading.

Jacob, the son of Isaac, the grandson of Abraham, the twin brother of Esau, the father of twelve sons by four wives had at least two memorable family reunions that are recorded in Genesis.

The first is when Jacob reunited with his brother Esau. As a young man, Jacob had run away from home for fear that his twin brother would kill him. Years later, not knowing whether his brother would still want to kill him and his family, he returned home. Happily, Esau had had equally good fortune and welcomed Jacob home with open arms. Genesis chapters 32 and 33 records this story.

The second is when Jacob, now an old man, and the rest of the family reunite with Joseph, his son. Up until this time, Jacob believed that Joseph was dead, killed by wild animals. Up until that time, Joseph's other brothers thought that he was out of their lives since they had sold him into slavery. Joseph, now second only to Pharaoh, welcomed the whole family back. Genesis chapters 42 through 46 records this story.

My little reunion pales in comparison to the two that occurred in Jacob's life. We had suffered from suicide, geographic separation, and dealing with my dad's new wife. Thankfully, we had not suffered from the kind of sibling rivalry Jacob was a part of both as a brother and as a father. My brothers and I had not been particularly close growing up, but we had not been jealous nor had there been fights of any kind.

## Personal Reflections

1. Describe a time when you have done more than you thought you were able to do.
2. Describe your life-changing cherished moments or experiences.

# Reflections from the Life of Christ

Jesus carried out His mission with exact precision. He had to be crucified during Passover week to become the Lamb of God. In order to do this, He had to get the Roman government leaders, the Jewish religious leaders, and the Jewish people to agree that He was a danger worthy of crucifixion during Passover week, not before, not after, but exactly on the Feast of the Passover.

# 25

# A SAFE AND HAPPY SHELTER

Dear Heavenly Father, let Your will be done in all that we do. Let us be faithful stewards of all You have provided for us. In Christ's name, amen.

August 2004, Age: 48

Dear Diary,

Hello from our new home on Bolsa Way. To be more precise, I should say, "Hello, from our ten-year-old home which is owned by the bank." The keys are ours, and we have started moving in. The first item that we moved in was our Bible.

Over the last few years, we had become increasingly unhappy with our home on Iris Street. In one instance, Paul had been pulled over by a cop, and instead of asking for his driver's license, the cop said, "What are you doing here?" He was obviously the wrong ethnicity for our neighborhood. When Paul answered, "I live a few houses down," the cop didn't believe him. Once his license verified the facts, the cop gave him a fix-it ticket that he deserved. Later Paul's car was broken into and another cop said, "Don't you have any equity in your house?" and advised him it was time to move. We didn't belong in our own neighborhood.

Fortunately, we had almost paid for it, and even though it was in the "wrong" neighborhood, it was still worth much more than we paid for over twenty years ago. Our decision to move was made after long hours of prayer and long hours of searching the Internet for just the right house. Paul and I prayed to God that, "Your will be done." We wanted to be sure that we weren't going where we shouldn't go. We wanted to be sure that we weren't spending what we shouldn't spend.

When we found the house on Bolsa Way, we both loved it on sight. All that we dreamed of did indeed exist. This was not a fixer upper. This house was already fixed up and nothing needed to be done. Once we made the decision to buy it, everything else started falling into place in record time, and now we are here! God has blessed us.

end of diary entry

## Speed Bump 25: A Safe and Happy Shelter

The great hymn "Beneath the Cross of Jesus" poetically describes the cross as a "safe and happy shelter," a "home within the wilderness," and a "trysting place where heaven's love and heaven's justice meet." The cross *is* our actual and only spiritual safe and happy shelter, but this speed bump is about the physical safe and happy shelter that was the house on Bolsa Way. The ability to live in its shelter was a huge blessing.

Genesis tells us the story of how God blesses Abraham, his son Isaac, his grandson Jacob, and his great grandchildren. Isaac's blessings are described in Genesis 26:12–13.

> Isaac planted crops in that land and the same year reaped a hundredfold, because the Lord blessed him. The man became rich, and his wealth continued to grow until he became very wealthy.

This passage has always stunned me. Isaac is not described as smart or wise or in any way whatever. He is just blessed. God is the giver, and Isaac is merely the receiver. Isaac is, however, a deserving receiver of God's gifts. The most memorable moment in his life must have been when he realized that his father was going to sacrifice him as God had commanded him. We aren't told how Isaac reacted to the prospect of being sacrificed, but I believe that Isaac had faith in God just as his father Abraham did. I think that Isaac's wealth and riches were God's blessing because of Isaac's faith in God.

It felt to us as if God had looked into our hearts and prepared the house of our dreams. We were living Psalm 37:4.

> Delight yourself in the Lord and he will give you the desires of your heart.

## Personal Reflections

1. What big decisions have you made quickly?
2. When did you ask for God's guidance?
3. When have you felt blessed by God?

# Reflections from the Life of Christ

In the Garden of Gethsemane, Jesus prayed, "Not my will, but thine be done." For Jesus, the answer was that God did will that He be crucified. For Jesus, the most faithful one of all time, the one most deserving of God's blessings on earth, for Jesus, the answer was that God willed Him to take the way of pain and suffering and not the way of ease and luxury.

# 26

## A Shooting Range

Dear Heavenly Father, grant those who are in the midst of marginalization, belittlement, and emotional terror the ability to endure it and the ability to escape it. In Christ's name, amen.

2005, Age: 49

Dear Diary,

This is a stunned, but not really surprised, April. It is the middle of the night. I just crawled back into bed after being awakened by my heart pounding to the point where I thought I might be having a heart attack. How did I ever get into this predicament?

I have been working for the same employer for almost seventeen years now, and I have had almost as many bosses. Every type of person has come along, young and old, male and female, easygoing and high energy, Chinese,

Japanese, Mexican, Italian, Caucasian, and I've worked easily alongside every one of them. Most of them realized right away that they could count on me to take care of whatever needed to be done and happily let me continue doing whatever I saw fit to do. For some of them, though, there was a "training" period, where they tried showing me that things were going to be different and that I was going to have to adjust to their standards, but this training period was always quite short. Soon, they found more interesting work to do themselves, and I was left alone to tend to the business in my own way.

My current boss has changed all that! I am his target. I've seen it happen many times and have wondered, "Why did so-and-so get targeted?" I could only imagine that somewhere some managers decided that that person needed to go, and since it is quite difficult to fire someone at a government job, what I call targeting is the method of choice.

It was immediately evident. The first step is marginalization. This new boss was my new boss for more than a month before he spoke to me. There were meetings, but I was left out. When I finally did meet him, it was because I ran into him in the hall, and it was apparent that he didn't want to meet me or talk to me. Well, I thought, his training period is going to be longer than normal.

The next step is belittlement. The biggest, most important project I had on my plate, when he came, was reporting to the state of California. The agency I worked for had requirements that had to be met. They were not them-selves difficult. The difficulty was translating the wording we used into the wording the state used and then figuring out how to gather the data to send to the state. At the request of the agency I worked for, I had spent quite some time defining and redefining those requirements so that we would be providing the state with more accurate data. At the end of that process, the agency I worked for responded with a formal thank-you letter. My boss responded with, "They thought you did a good job."

The next step is torture, not physical torture, but rather mental torture. At the end of one of these torture ses-sions, one of my work associates said, "Take away the physical torture in an episode of *24* and what we just experienced was just as painful." During these torture sessions, also known as status meetings, I made it my goal to stay calm, not whine, and kept my statements as short and factual as possible.

Up until now, I've managed marginally well, during my waking hours, that is. As I lie in my bed though, still wide awake, I know that what happened this morning was that in my sleep, I was running away. I was running as fast as I could and as far away as I could get. That is why my heart was pounding. I can control the day, but I can't control the night. I know, now, that I have got to get another job or another boss or I'll die.

end of diary entry

# Speed Bump 26: A Shooting Range

I had walked right into a shooting range, and I was the target.

Throughout these years, my goal had been to be recognized as a programmer, and without any doubt, that is what happened. The programmers all worked for a division, and that division basically contracted out their programmers to the different agencies. The agency that I was contracted out to was the same for all the years I worked there, and the person that I worked for at the agency was there throughout most of my career there. When she left, that's when the trouble started, and when a boss came along who did not know anything about her came along, that's when I was in big trouble. This is exactly the situation that the Israelites faced at the beginning of Exodus.

> Now Joseph and all his brothers and all that generation died, but the Israelites were fruitful and multiplied greatly and became exceedingly numerous, so that the land was filled with them. Then a new king, *who did not know about Joseph*, came to power in Egypt. "Look," he said to his people, "the Israelites have become much too numerous for us. Come, we must deal shrewdly with them or they will become even more numerous and, if war breaks out, will join our enemies, fight against us and leave the country." So, they put slave masters over them to oppress them with forced labor. (Exodus 1:6–11a)

The key is that the king did not know anything about how Joseph had saved Egypt from the famine that struck the whole area surrounding Egypt about four hundred years earlier. Joseph and his family had been welcomed into Egypt as saviors and been given the best of everything. Now their descendants were being treated as if they were scum.

## Personal Reflections

1. Have you had a boss from hell, and if so, how did you deal with him/her?
2. Have you had other team members from hell, and how did you deal with them?
3. Have you been targeted by someone in a non-work setting?
4. Have you suddenly gone from being well-liked to being disliked?

# Reflections from the Life of Christ

When Jesus comes into Jerusalem for His last time, He is hailed by the crowds as "The king of Israel." In less than a week, these same crowds will shout, "Crucify Him! Crucify Him!"

# 27

## UNCHARTED TERRITORY

Dear Heavenly Father, be with those who are dealing with unanticipated, radical change in their lives and who find themselves unsure and off-balance. In Christ's name, amen.

May 2006, Age: 50

Dear Diary,

I am fifty years old. I have taken early retirement. I have just finished my first day working for a private company in Camarillo. It's all happened so fast.

I first tried going right to my customers once I knew I had to get away from my boss. My idea was that I would just tell them that I could work directly for them instead of working through the middleman. That way, I could get rid of my boss and work directly for my customers. That was a lousy idea. Once I offered that as an option, I was told never to speak to anyone unless I had an agenda prepared in advance and unless I kept to the agenda. This further cut me off. Now my boss and my customers were unhappy with me.

The next thing I tried was going directly to my boss's boss and seeing if I could transfer away from my boss. After all, people did it all the time. Why not me? When I offered that as an option, I was told that no one else wanted me and I should just continue working for my boss.

And then one day, I was walking out with some of my coworkers when one of them mentioned that she had a friend who needed help. The job description for the position he needed to fill almost exactly matched my work experience. That is how I wound up working for a private company in Camarillo. But best of all, I was able to work at my old job until reaching exactly fifty years old, the magical age when early retirement is available. My retirement pay is nothing but a stipend, but it is a stipend that will last the rest of my life.

I'm so grateful that I have this new job, but at the same time, I am terrified. Is this fire to the frying pan? What am I doing at fifty years old changing jobs? What am I doing moving from the public sector to the private sector? This is almost never done due to the perception by those in the private sector that those in the public sector have cushy jobs. It only happened to me because of the friendship between my friend and the private sector boss. Her words had weight, but that was her, now it is up to me to deliver.

Even though I have prayed continuously to find a way to get away from my boss and God has delivered, it isn't what I want. I want my old job back, the way it was before my bully boss arrived there. I want to stay there until I reach the age to receive a full retirement check.

end of diary entry

## Speed Bump 27: Uncharted Territory

I had found my way out of the shooting range, but where was I exactly? Uncharted territory.

I was acting just exactly like the Israelites acted when they left Egypt only to find that the Canaanites were powerful. Egypt, like my old job, was terrible. What the Israelites really wanted was for God to save them from the Egyptians by conquering the Egyptians. They didn't want to conquer Canaan. That was a big new job.

> That night all the people of the community raised their voices and wept aloud. All the Israelites grumbled against Moses and Aaron, and the whole assembly said to them, "If only we had died in Egypt! Or in this desert! Why is the Lord bringing us to this land only to let us fall by the sword? Our wives and children will be taken as plunder. Wouldn't it be better for us to go back to Egypt?" And they said to each other, "We should choose a leader and *go back to Egypt*." (Numbers 14:1–4)

The cries of the Israelites echoed my own. Why did God put me in a position where I would encounter a bully boss who was intent upon getting rid of me? They were ready to run back home to Egypt, and I was wishing I could go back to my old job. Another famous, Old Testament person in a similar position is Elijah.

> Now Ahab told Jezebel everything Elijah had done and how he had killed all the prophets with the sword. So Jezebel sent a messenger to Elijah to say, "May the gods deal with me, be it ever so severely, if by this time tomorrow I do not make your life like that of one of them." Elijah was afraid and ran for his life. When he came to Beersheba in Judah, he left his servant there, while he himself went a day's journey into the desert. He came to a broom tree, sat down under it and prayed that he might die. "I have had enough, Lord," he said, *"Take my life;* I am no better than my ancestors." Then he lay down under the tree and fell asleep. (1 Kings 19:1–5)

Elijah was in such bad shape that he asked God to take his life rather than continue living with his new reality of facing the wrath of Jezebel.

## Personal Reflections

1. Have you trusted God to take care of the bullies in your life?
2. Have you decided to take advantage of new opportunities sent by God?
3. Are you currently suffering under the attack of bullies?

## Reflections from the Life of Christ

As a matter of fact, Jesus did face radical change. For starters He changed from His existence as a spiritual body, in very nature God, to a human baby boy! Now that is a radical change!

# 28

## A Planned/Unplanned Meeting

Dear Heavenly Father, be with those who grieve over the aging of friends and family. Be with those who have entered the final stages of their lives. In Christ's name, amen.

Summer 2008, Age: 52

Dear Diary,

Hello from Alaska! I am on a cruise with Paul, my father, and his wife. This is not any old cruise. We have booked our cruise as part of a group of Focus on the Family radio program listeners. I have not been a listener or monetary supporter of Focus on the Family, too busy working, but my father has been, and Paul and I are along for the ride.

Paul and I have just had our picture taken with Dr. James Dobson and his wife as part of a meet and greet. We shook their hands, chitchatted for a few seconds, smiled, had our picture taken, and have moved on. Dr. Dobson and his wife are obviously full of integrity. I don't know when I've ever felt such peace as what I felt from each of them. And we are just one couple out of hundreds that they will meet and greet today.

My father and his wife are right behind us now. For years, my dad has been saying that, "This will be my last vacation," but we all know that this really will be his last vacation. He walks with a cane, but not like anyone I've ever seen before who walks with a cane. His bad leg doesn't work at all. His cane is a substitute leg. He needs to be using a walker, but he tells us that when he is ready, he'll use a walker, but for now, all he needs is a cane. It is clearly not enjoyable for him to walk anymore, but he doesn't complain, he is just slow.

We have been on many vacations together. The Grand Canyon trip was such a grand experience and the start of other much less grand but still memorable experiences. He would drive down, stay for a few days, and during his stay, I would take time off work. We would get in my car and travel all around Southern California. We took a few day trips to the Channel Islands and did some whale watching a few times. Sometimes we got ambitious and stayed at Las Vegas or Reno. He would always come by himself, leaving his wife behind.

Over the last few years, he's not been willing to leave her behind, and the two of them have made a few trips to visit. These visits were a little awkward and harder to manage, but so long as I got to see my dad every so often, I was happy. I'm not sure whose idea it was, but several years ago, we decided to go on a cruise to Hawaii together, all four of us. I was a little uncertain how that would go, but we did have a marvelous time. We followed that up with a fly-drive trip to South Dakota, which was equally marvelous, and now, Alaska.

I couldn't help but think that this moment is a perfectly fitting period to the end of the sentence of this stage in my dad's life. My father, the man famous in his daughter's eyes, shakes hands with Dr. Dobson, the famous Focuser on the Family. In my mind's eye, I saw fireworks going off in the distance as angels clapped their hands over the two of them shaking hands. I had felt the integrity flowing from Dr. Dobson. Did Dr. Dobson feel the integrity flowing from my dad?

I know that my dad is flawed, but in this moment, it is not about his flaws, it is about his greatness. I saw the man who had been my hero, who had sacrificed so much for me and his whole family. Work, for him, had not been about making money or making a name for himself, but rather about making ends meet. Although there were many opportunities for him to work overtime, he didn't take them. It was not worth it to spend any extra time at work and deprive his family of the time we all loved spending with him.

end of diary entry

# Speed Bump 28: A Planned/ Unplanned Meeting

This speed bump made me stop. I knew I would. That was no surprise. It was a planned meeting. The agenda was clearly known well before it happened, and yet, as is so often the case, there were unknown agenda items for this meeting.

First, there was the stated agenda item of meeting and greeting Dr. and Mrs. Dobson. The Israelites of Solomon's time heard God's cheering when they finished building His temple. They were, in a sense, having a meet and greet between themselves and God.

> When Solomon finished praying, fire came down from heaven and consumed the burnt offering and the sacrifices and the glory of the Lord filled the temple. The priests could not enter the temple of the Lord because the glory of the Lord filled it. When all the Israelites saw the fire coming down and the glory of the Lord above the temple, they knelt on the pavement with their faces to the ground, and they worshipped and gave thanks to the Lord, saying, "He is good; his love endures forever." (2 Chronicles 7:1–3)

In the moments when God truly cheers, everyone knows. In this case though, I was the only one that thought that the meeting of my dad and Dr. Dobson was anything but a handshake among hundreds. To Dr. Dobson, my father was just another hand to shake. To my dad, this was just one more reason to stand when all he wanted to do was sit. This was the true significance of this moment. It was clear that my dad didn't care whether he met Dr. Dobson or not. My dad had reached the point in his life where he didn't want to stand in line for anything or anyone. This man who had been an usher at his local church, greeting people and making them welcome, didn't care whether he met or greeted another person, famous or not.

The second, unknown agenda item for this meeting was the meet and greet where I met for the first time with my aged, physically frail, father. The man who had wielded an axe and chainsaw with ease as a young man could not stand now without the aid of a cane. It hurt to see my father this way. Did Jesus hurt to see His father age? We don't know what happened to Joseph, and we know that Jesus' Father, God, does not age. However, consider the passage where Jesus describes His family.

> When Jesus was still talking to the crowd, his mother and brothers stood outside, wanting to speak to him. Someone told him, "Your mother and brothers are standing outside, wanting to speak to you." He replied to him, "Who is my mother, and who are my brothers?" Pointing to his disciples, he said, "*Here are my mother and my brothers.* For whoever does the will of my Father in heaven is my brother and sister and mother." (Matthew 12:46–50)

## Personal Reflections

1. Have you watched as your loved ones move into the next phase of their lives?
2. Have you ever heard, in your mind's eye anyway, heavenly cheering?

# Reflections from the Life of Christ

Does Jesus care about my aging father? Yes, He considers my father to be His brother. Just imagine all the pain He suffers while watching all His brothers age and all His sisters agonizing over it.

# 29

## THE FAST LANE

Dear Heavenly Father, please give those who see no way out of their particular unhappy circumstances a ray of hope and a means to live life to its fullest. In Christ's name, amen.

2009, Age: 53

Dear Diary,

I just got home from the first day of my new life as an Oxnard, California, to Woodland Hills, California, commuter. The alarm clock went off at 7:00 AM. I was on the road before 8:00 AM. Traffic slowed to a halt two times, but I arrived to work a little before scheduled to, at 9:00 AM. Scenes alongside the 101 freeway, also known as the Ventura Freeway, passed by without any fanfare. At 6:00 PM, I left my Woodland Hills office in Los Angeles County and returned home at 7:00 PM. From 7:00 AM to 7:00 PM devoted exclusively to work is going to be how life is for the foreseeable future. How did I get myself into this mess?

One year ago, I went to work just as I had so many days before and turned on my computer, opened my e-mail, and there it was. Our little company was being bought by a big company. The e-mail assured us that all our jobs were safe and that this acquisition was about growth and not about layoffs or job losses. The big company had its offices in Woodland Hills, and eventually, all of us would be working at the Woodland Hills location.

My first reaction was disbelief. Surely it just was a hoax or someone's idea of a big joke, but the e-mail was followed by a company-wide meeting where we were told that no, this is not a hoax, yes, it is very real and it is very good and all our jobs were safe, and no, there are no exceptions. *Everyone's* job location will move to Woodland Hills.

My next reaction was to immediately start looking for another job. There was no way I was ever going to spend twelve hours a day devoted to working. That was not going to happen! Through the grapevine, I had learned that my old boss, who had caused me so much trouble, had moved on to another job. Furthermore, I knew that my old job was looking for someone to fill the position I had when I left. I would just get my old job back!

However, I did not succeed in getting my old job back or in finding another job despite my best efforts. I did not get my old job back even though I knew exactly who to talk to and what to do and followed up in all the right ways. The official response to my interview was a letter which in effect said that I was not qualified to do my old job. Ouch, but with that letter, I found out that the whole management, not just my old boss, didn't want me to work there. Who cared about them anyway? Certainly not me! I would just get some other job! I had an entire year to find something, but in that entire year, I only applied for one position. They interviewed me and decided to hire someone else.

There is no other option but commuting. I had prayed without ceasing, hoping this day would never come, hoping I would not have to commute, but here I am, commuting. I taught my last piano lesson last week. Since I won't be home until about 7:00 PM, there's no way to figure out how to schedule piano lessons. I had been attending the midweek Bible study at our church, but now I will not be home in time to go there. For the first time in my working life, work will be all I have time to do during the workweek. I'm resigned to it, but it is going to be torture!

end of diary entry

## Speed Bump 29: The Fast Lane

I had made it to the fast lane, literally. One very costly speeding ticket was all I needed to slow down and move over a lane or two, but I was still on the work fast lane with no life except work. It was intolerable the first day, the first year, the second year, and never ceased being intolerable, but I kept doing it because I had to do it. I needed the money. I was in a bind with no idea how to get out of it. There was no way that I could get another equally good paying job. I was stuck in the fast lane! There was nothing I could do but endure it!

My biggest question was, "How long?" Moses poses a similar question to Pharaoh.

> So Moses and Aaron went to Pharaoh and said to him, "This is what the Lord, the God of the Hebrews, says: '*How long* will you refuse to humble yourself before me? Let my people go, so that they may worship me. If you refuse to let them go, I will bring locusts into your country tomorrow.'" (Exodus 10:3–4)

For Moses and Aaron, the question was how long before the Israelites would be able to quit being slaves to the Egyptians. For me, the question was how long before I would be able to quit spending two hours a day going back and forth to work.

Samson's story tells of a man living in a real grind.

> Then the Philistines seized him, gouged out his eyes and took him down to Gaza. Binding him with bronze shackles, they *set him to grinding* in the prison. (Judges 16:21)

Samson had been a judge who had saved his people from the Philistines and had the misfortune to be in love with a wicked woman who turned him in to the Philistines. My fake, air-conditioned, hour-long grind paled in comparison to his real, sweat-producing, lifelong grind.

## Personal Reflections

1. Did you ever find yourself working longer hours than you wanted?
2. How well do you manage your time?
3. Given my situation, what would you do?

## Reflections from the Life of Christ

In an outburst similar to my own, Jesus said,
"O unbelieving and perverse generation, how
long shall I stay with you? How long shall
I put up with you?" (Matthew 17:17).
Just being on earth was an unbelievably
long and difficult grind for Jesus.

# 30

## A RIVER

Dear Heavenly Father, please provide healing balm for those whose hearts are breaking. In Christ's name, amen.

December 2010, Age: 54

Dear Diary,

I am weeping. This isn't just a few tears that will soon be over. These are "cry me a river" tears. I wasn't expecting to cry. I thought I was tough and prepared for the events of this day, but obviously, I am not either tough or prepared.

It all started with one of my weekly phone calls to my dad, who is living in Mesa, Arizona, now. Our calls had been quite short, mostly filled with obligatory assurances that everything was fine during recent months as both my dad's and stepmom's health had been deteriorating. My stepmother, on this occasion, however, answered, and I said, "How are you?" After a long pause, unusual for her, she said, "Mad." What followed was a description of an unbelievable hospital stay which I am unable to retell with any degree of certainty. What was clear though was that her daughter, my stepsister who lives in Mesa, had attempted to kill her! At first, I tried reasoning with her. Her daughter brought her safely home from the hospital. If she wanted to kill her mother, that would have been the perfect opportunity. It was hopeless, though. My stepmom's mind was made up. She and my father were going to move away from the daughter she was now terrified by, to the safety of two of her other daughters, in Texas! She informed me that steps were already being taken to make it happen as soon as possible!

All of us hoped that in a very short time, my stepmother would realize that her daughter did not attempt to kill her, but this delusion continued, caused by the infection that was the reason for her hospital stay in the first place. I had planned a visit there a few weeks after the now-infamous hospital stay, but after my visit with them, I determined that there was no hope for the relationship. My stepmother was still adamant that her daughter had meant her harm and that they had to get away from Mesa.

Soon after that, we all gathered together in Mesa for my stepmother's eightieth birthday. Her daughter from Australia had made all the arrangements for a birthday celebration. The two daughters from Texas came, one with a new husband and the other with her son. The daughter from Mesa was there, even though she was cut to the core over her situation, with some of her children and one grandchild. Paul and I were there too. The plan was for us all to have brunch and then for my father and stepmother to get in the car with one of the daughters from Texas as soon as brunch was over and begin their long drive to Dallas, Texas.

I was fine up until the moment when my father got into the car to leave Arizona. At that moment, I started to cry and made a hasty path to our car where I am now watching as they leave for Dallas. I know that their life in Mesa cannot work anymore and that the move to Dallas will hopefully be for the best, but still, it won't be possible for us to just get in the car and drive to Dallas over a weekend. Logically, it is the best way, but my heart is breaking, and I feel as if I am a mother watching as her child has just left home. My father uses a wheelchair all the time, and getting into and out of a car is a hard job for him. My stepmother's back hurts all the time, and I worry that she will be terribly uncomfortable sitting in the backseat of a car during the road trip to Dallas. My stepmother has decided to quit driving once they get to Dallas, and I worry whether she will successfully make that transition. Most of all, I will miss being able to see them as often as I have been lately.

Memories of my childhood and especially my father's quiet influence flood through my mind as I fight to hold back the tears. For a Father's Day gift a few years ago, I had written a few paragraphs about him and asked a friend from church to turn it into a poem. When I gave it to my father, he refused to believe the poem was even about him until he came to the last stanza which identifies him by name. I could tell that he was happy with the way I had described him, and I was pleased that the framed poem made its way to the wall in his bedroom.

### Memories of My Father

In kindergarten, toppling off the monkey bars I went
So to the principal's office my dad was sent
What a relief to be scooped up by his big arm
I knew then I was safe again from any more harm

In Olivehurst, riding our bikes was such a thrill
As a family we went up and down each hill
Falling, we got right back up feeling no fear
Riding those old dirt roads, we felt like a pioneer

We moved to Penryn building a home to our glee
Right in the middle of a plum orchard and many a tree
Granite outcroppings, bushes, buckeye, and big oak
Playing tag and building a fort made us feel like magical folk

Making grass houses with rooms and
hallways was so much fun
Then out of the fields to the surrounding forest we would run

SPEED BUMPS ON THE WAY TO HEAVEN

A little stream, clay mines, and a natural
sandbox became our own
Dorothy had Oz, Alice had Wonderland
… we had magic at our home

Out the kitchen window and top of
the hill laid a panoramic view
An old granite quarry, a big hole, and
mineshaft gave us lots to do
Dreaming of gold miners, our "railroad
country" became the new name
We were in our own "Wonderland" as
we played each and every game

Heating during the winter cold was
difficult as dollars were few
Dad took his chainsaw, shovel, and axe
to the plum trees to make do
We held the pieces as Dad would saw,
stacking the wood so neat
The big fireplace in the family room
kept us warm from head to feet

Assisting Dad sort soda bottles, we learned the value of work
In the local grocery store he stocked
shelves of food as a retail clerk
Being alongside our dad was fun and
never seemed to us a chore
Whatever task he gave us, we completed
cheerfully and asked for more

Memories of family road trips to
destinations that seemed so far

"Are we there yet?" was the constant
question as we rode in the car
The temperatures in the hundreds during summer were so hot
Going to the beach, removing shoes
and socks, was the coolest spot

We walked along the sand without a care
as the ocean rushed to and fro
Until a strong wave knocked me over
and into the undertow I did go
Again my dad's strong arms picked me up and held me near
When I was scared, he was always there to remove all fear

Dad tried his best to teach me sports, but that was not to be
Hitting, catching a ball, and running
the bases were not easy for me
Finally, a left-handed catcher's mitt
was the answer to our prayer
My dad pitched so perfectly that the ball just landed there

Music and playing piano became the thing I would love
Dad drove me to lessons and said I
played like an angel from above
He endured my many failures and successes
as I banged out my tunes
While he tried to watch his sports on
TV and rest in the afternoons

My dad never complained and was always the best
In my struggles growing up, he helped me with every test
Those bonds we built—daughter and dad—will always last
I will miss him so much when from this life he has passed

Having such a wonderful, strong, earthly father to love
Made it easy to believe in a supreme heavenly Father above
I thank God for blessing me with such a dad
Dale McCorkle—greatest father a daughter ever had

Written by Linda Howard
For April Vider
April 2010

end of diary entry

## Speed Bump 30: A River

I pretty much cried a river of tears all the way from Mesa, Arizona, to Oxnard, California, that day. I knew there wasn't any hope that the move would be anything but difficult. Furthermore, I knew there wasn't any hope that any other moving or staying would be any less difficult. It was complicated! Too complicated to ever be anything other than complicated!

The Old Testament story of Jonathan and David most closely parallels this point in my life. Jonathan and David, at this point in their story, know that Jonathan's father, King Saul, intends to kill David.

After the boy had gone, David got up from the south side of the stone, and bowed down before Jonathan three times, with his face to the ground. They kissed each other and *wept together*—but David wept the most. Jonathan said to David,

"Go in peace, for we have sworn friendship with each other in the name of the Lord, saying, 'The Lord is witness between you and me, and between your descendants and my descendants forever.'" Then David left, and Jonathan went back to the town. (1 Samuel 20:41–42)

David, the future king, and Jonathan, the prince who would never be king are in a friendship that cannot be but is. David must move away, actually run for his life, and they both know it, and it breaks their hearts.

## Personal Reflections

1. Have you had to deal with aging parents?
2. Have you had to watch as those you love move away?

## Reflections from the Life of Christ

Was Jesus ever overwhelmed with sorrow over a family member? Yes. Every child who has attended Sunday school for any length of time will know the shortest verse in the Bible is "Jesus wept." He wept over the death of Lazarus, whom He thought of as a brother.

# AFTERWORD

Cleaning the closet would have to wait for another time. I folded the suicide notes back up, careful to fold the paper only where my mother had folded. I did not want to introduce any fold that was not done with her hands. Then I placed them back in the box labeled "MOM" and returned the box to its place in the closet.

It is good to be retired and able to think through my life's speed bumps and put them into some kind of perspective. The story of how I retired is such a good one, but one that I haven't had time yet to digest. Perhaps later I will write that one down.

You know now that there is nothing extraordinary about me and my Christian faith. I don't have a degree in theology and didn't even go to a Christian college. I am an ordinary Christian, stumbling and bumbling through my ordinary Christian life.

Chances are, you are an ordinary Christian too. As we have thought about our lives together, you and I, I know I have found that the miniscule difficulties I have had pale in comparison to what He went through. I suspect you have discovered, probably rediscovered, that as well. It is, after all, not about us and what we have gone through; it is about Him and what He has gone through for us.

No matter what speed bumps are ahead, let us keep taking Christ and Christianity with us as we altogether strive to reach our ultimate heavenly goal. Heaven, we are on our way to heaven! A crown of glory awaits us there. Until we celebrate our arrival there, let us keep cherishing that old rugged cross and never forgetting the ways that God led Him to heaven.

On a hill far away
Stood an old rugged cross
The emblem of suffering and shame

And I love that old cross
Where the dearest and best
For a world of lost sinners was slain

So I'll cherish the old rugged cross
Till my trophies at last I lay down
I will cling to the old rugged cross
And exchange it someday for a crown.

# ABOUT THE AUTHOR

April Vider has lived in some region of California her whole life. She was raised in the small Northern California town of Penryn, but for most of her adult life, she has been a resident of Southern California.

She graduated from California State University, Long Beach, in 1979 with a bachelor's of arts degree in history and then proceeded to work in information technology for over thirty years. She retired in 2014.

Her real passion, during her working years, was her work for God and His church, first learning, then teaching the Bible. She has been teaching Bible school for children between first and eighth grades since the 1980s.

Retirement has allowed her to continue her service as a Bible schoolteacher for children and to take up many of her other interests. She began teaching a woman's Bible study group. She is devoting more of her time to piano teaching and piano playing/accompanying. She and her husband of over thirty years, Paul, who is also retired, especially like taking short trips around the great state of California, which offers such a wide variety of destinations, including desert, beach, and mountains, all within a few hours from their home in Oxnard, California. And last but not least, she is finally adding writing Christian women's books to the list of her many pursuits.

CPSIA information can be obtained
at www.ICGtesting.com
Printed in the USA
FSHW010418230821
84232FS